Changes in Health Care

Reflections on the NHS Internal Market

Edited by
Paul Anand
and
Alistair McGuire

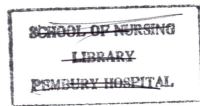

MACMILLAN
Business

First published 1997 by
MACMILLAN PRESS LTD
Houndmills, Basingstoke, Hampshire RG21 6XS
and London
Companies and representatives
throughout the world

ISBN 0–333–63420–9

A catalogue record for this book is available
from the British Library.

This book is printed on paper suitable for recycling and
made from fully managed and sustained forest sources.

10 9 8 7 6 5 4 3 2 1
06 05 04 03 02 01 00 99 98 97

Printed and bound in Great Britain by
Antony Rowe Ltd
Chippenham, Wiltshire

WX 120

WX 139

NHS   HEALTH ECON

PURCHASING INTERNAL MARKET
CONTRACTS FIN
MAN

CHANGES IN HEALTH CARE

Contents

Acknowledgements

All the papers in this volume have been refereed. The editors wish to thank those involved in this process: Will Bartlett (University of Bristol), Gwyn Bevan (University of Bristol), Maria Goddard (NHS), David Cohen (University of Glamorgan), Ann-Marie Craig (University of St Andrews), Brenda Leese (University of York), Robert G. Milne (University of Glasgow), Christopher McCabe (University of Sheffield), Douglas McCulloch (University of Ulster at Jordanstown), John W. Posnett (University of York), Adrian Towse (Office of Health Economics) and Sara Twaddle (Greater Glasgow Health Board).

Notes on the Contributors

Paul Anand is Reader in Decision Theory at De Montfort University. He is managing editor of *Risk Decision and Policy*, has held posts at Oxford, Cambridge and York Universities and has acted as consultant to a number of organisations, including the OECD, the NHS and Arthur Andersen. Current research interests include foundations of decision theory, health policy, government management of risk and the economic/social/organisational implications of the internet.

Cam Donaldson is Professor of Health Economics at the University of Aberdeen. His current interests are in willingness to pay for health care, health care financing and health care priority setting. Recent publications include *Can We Afford the NHS?*, published by the Institute for Public Policy Research.

Lesley Griffiths is Lecturer in Health Policy and Medical Sociology in the Department of Nursing, Midwifery and Health Care at the University of Wales, Swansea. Her current interests include the organisation of community mental health services, NHS contracts and interprofessional working.

David Hughes is Reader in Health Policy in the Department of Nursing, Midwifery and Health Care at the University of Wales, Swansea. His current research interests include NHS contracts, management discourses, rationing and evidence-based purchasing.

David Hunter is Director of the Nuffield Institute for Health and Professor of Health Policy and Management at the University of Leeds. He is also a non-executive director of Leeds Health Authority. His interests are in rationing healthcare, accountability, the limits to evidence-based medicine and European health systems reform.

Duncan Keeley is a General Practitioner in Thame, Oxfordshire, and a member of the General Practice and Primary Care Advisory Committee of Oxfordshire Health Authority.

Alistair McGuire is Professor of Health Economics at City University, London, and a Research Associate in the Oxford Health Economics

Group. Prior to this he was at the Centre for Socio-Legal Studies, Wolfson College, and taught at Pembroke College, Oxford. He is co-ordinator of the MSc in Economic and Quantitative Methods in Health Care at City University. He has acted as an adviser to the UK Cabinet Office, the World Health Organisation and a number of pharmaceutical companies on health economics. He has written widely in the area, and his current interests are in contracts, hospital economics and economic evaluation.

Jean McHale is Lecturer in the Faculty of Law and a director of the Centre for Social Ethics and Policy at the University of Manchester. Her current and recent research interests include NHS contracts, medical confidentiality and whistle-blowing, ethical and legal issues in rationing, and nursing law.

Russell Mannion is Department of Health Research Fellow in the Centre for Health Economics at the University of York. His principal research interests are the financing of health care and the evaluation of health and social care markets.

Annabelle Mark is Lecturer at South Bank and Middlesex Universities. Her teaching, writing and research interests include organisational behaviour and health care management. She spent ten years as a manager in the NHS.

Gavin Mooney is Professor of Health Economics at the University of Sydney. His current research interests include health care priority setting, aboriginal health, community values and equity. He is currently co-editing a book on the economics of Australian health policy.

Penelope Mullen is Senior Lecturer in the Health Services Management Centre, University of Birmingham. Her teaching and research interests include health policy, planning, rationing, priority setting, information and quantitative analysis.

Peter Smith is Professor in the Department of Economics and the Centre for Health Economics at the University of York. His principal research interests are the financing of health care and the measurement of efficiency in the public sector.

1 Introduction: evaluating health care reform

Alistair McGuire and Paul Anand

INTRODUCTION

Economists argue that government intervention should begin with an analysis of the institutional failure it seeks to remedy, though politicians often start elsewhere. In the second half of the 1980s the Conservative government became increasingly interested in the application of market-type mechanisms to transactions within the National Health Service, and by 1991 it had introduced to the service reforms hailed as the most substantial since its inception. The major instrument of these reforms was the creation of a market internal to the NHS premised on a clear separation between purchasers and providers of health care.

On one level it appears that the health care sector reforms have been driven by the desire to contain health care costs rather than to promote economic efficiency *per se*. Possible motives include pressures on public sector resources and a belief that the public purse (in many countries) is increasingly funding commodities that provide individualistic benefits whilst moving away from traditional public goods. The consequence is that public sectors which have recently experienced increased growth over and above the underlying growth rate of prices and/or national income have come under particular scrutiny. In this environment attention has inevitably been drawn to the health care sector.

Even if cost containment is the primary objective, judgements may also be made of the relative efficiency of competing forms of organisation. This involves consideration of the various means by which health care can be financed and delivered. The question of the means of delivery of any commodity may be formulated as follows: because resources are scarce society has to make choices over their use, and while this is most commonly achieved by means of market allocation, there are competing institutions which are capable of allocating resources,

1

for example command or hierarchy, or more generally through public provision. The relative efficiency of these means of allocation is to be judged by their relative disadvantages and merits, that is by their relative costs and benefits.

Every form of health care system has both efficiency and inefficiency impacts – costs as well as benefits. The choice amongst the mix ought ultimately to be dictated by empirical considerations. This is rarely the case, however, given the difficulties involved in testing one system against another. Indeed no direct empirical evidence exists to support an argument for or against any particular form of *system*. A further complication is that each system is liable to have its own different institutional idiosyncrasies and must be considered within its own historical and cultural setting. In analysing the broad efficiency questions that must be addressed it is recognised that the approach is simplistic in the extreme, even so it is apparent that there is no simple *a priori* answer to the question of which form of organisation ought to be accepted.

In this opening chapter we seek to describe, therefore, the fundamentals of the internal market, not as an end in itself but rather as an instrument to the achievement of certain goals that seem to be widely shared. The aim is to compare what we know about the effects of the reforms with the kind of institutional failures that apparently motivated their introduction.

THE INTERNAL MARKET

The internal market characterised as the interaction between purchasers, acting as agents on behalf of a defined population, and providers, was considered to be a vehicle for major changes in the production and delivery of health care in the UK. The market, it was supposed, would allow purchasers the opportunity to be innovative in selecting which services to buy on behalf of their population. In addition, some providers, particularly those hospitals opting for independent trust status, would be able to develop new markets for their services. The change in incentives as the system moved from being administered to market led was seen by many as introducing dynamics into a rather moribund and constrained organisation (see McGuire, Fenn and Mayhew, 1991).

Operationally, however, the transition has not been as powerful as many had imagined. There has been considerable activity in re-structuring the sector. Some have argued that the major impact may be on the administrative costs of operating a market (Quam, 1991). Nonetheless, a majority of hospitals and General Practices have now established their own management structures through hospital trust or GP fund-holding practices. This has been a major achievement of the NHS reforms and can be interpreted as an extension of the desire to establish effective management structures within the NHS which began with *The Griffiths Report* (HMSO, 1983). These proposals stressed the need for a clearer delegation of responsibility and accountability in the process of allocating health sector resources. They initiated a reorganisation which emphasised functional management and clear lines of responsibility and certainly progress towards the latter has been achieved with the semi-autonomous units created by trusts and GP fund-holding.

Changes in actual production and delivery of health care have hardly been so dramatic. For one thing, changes in organisational structure have little impact on resource allocation unless the appropriate environmental conditions are attained. These conditions depend critically on the actual operation of the contractual relationships which determine the incentives, and therefore the behaviour of both purchasers and providers.

Contract specification and operation

Three types of contract exist: block contracts, cost and volume contracts and cost per case contracts. Essentially these differ in the extent to which individual items of service (e.g., a hospital in-patient case of a given diagnostic category) are separately identified and paid for. The block contract is akin to the pre-reform arrangement: the hospital provides access to its capacity in exchange for a lump sum prospective payment. Typically, the block contract is slightly more complex with lower and upper ceilings on patient numbers specified. Any significant pre-specified deviation could lead to a re-negotiation of financial terms (Appleby *et al.*, 1994). The cost and volume contract involves a fixed payment to treat patients up to a given volume above which the reimbursement is case-related (usually up to an upper limit). Finally the cost per case contract is fully dependent on the actual provider workload. Clearly, the higher the proportion of a provider's activity which is paid for on a block contract basis, the higher will be the proportion of fixed to variable revenue reported by that provider.

While the supporters of the internal market hoped cost and volume and cost per case contracts would quickly become the norm in terms of contract specification, currently block contracts dominate. Moreover, contracting tends to reflect established patterns of service provision. The main exceptions to this rule are the fund-holding general practices, which have, in some locations, negotiated new forms of service provision, or opted to provide additional services themselves (Crump *et al.*, 1991).

Some have argued that there are good reasons to expect block contracts to remain the common form of contractual arrangement in the internal market. When there is a capacity constraint on the provision of services the provider may seek to assure themselves of part of this capacity by maintaining a block contract. Competition from GP fundholders and other Trusts increase the likelihood of maintaining block contracts. The potential risk arises that the purchaser may overestimate the capacity constraints they face and, through the block contract, pay for unutilised health care (Fenn, Rickman and McGuire, 1994). Capacity constraints may distort competition. When provider capacity is constrained, as is likely to be the case in any particular area at any particular point in time, the purchaser may be prepared to pay a premium to secure such capacity for their population in the form of a block contract. Obviously as capacity grows this premium is weakened. The impact of provider competition will rely therefore, to some extent, on the capacity existing within the sector. The irony of competition is that in the short run it may lead to capacity reductions, which over time could lead to purchasers increasing reimbursement to secure scarcer capacity in the longer term. The administrative and transaction costs of specifying block contracts may also be lower than those arising from other forms of contract.

With all three types of contract it is necessary to determine the service priorities, to specify the contract clearly in terms of what will be delivered, of a given quality at an agreed price, and to monitor performance. There are substantial operational difficulties with each of these components. Health sector objectives are rarely specified. The regulation of price and its relationship to both volume and quality of output is difficult. The mechanisms which remedy failure in the exchange process are not explicitly defined. In short, the optimal structural conditions for the operation of contracts, and therefore the internal market, are not known.

The fundamental basis of the contracting process is the operation of a specific pricing mechanism which aims to provide both information and incentives to ensure resources are allocated efficiently. Yet efficiency is merely a means to an end, and the end has to be defined before an appropriate pricing mechanism can be designed. Thus no pricing rules can be designed until the objectives of the health care system are known. A basic flaw of the NHS internal market is that a specific pricing rule, essentially based on (normally short run) average costs, has been adopted yet the objectives have not been defined explicitly. Thus, as is so often the case in public policy, we have to infer what those objectives are and presume that they are the appropriate ones to strive for.

Basic economic principles indicate that efficient prices (prices that determine the optimal level of output), must be equal to marginal costs. In other words, to implement efficient allocation, the price a purchaser pays for additional output must equal the cost borne by the provider of producing that additional output – the marginal cost. The short run average cost only relates to marginal cost if output can be increased at constant cost, that is, if the cost of producing a unit of output does not vary with the number of outputs produced. If this holds true, then short run average costs will always equal marginal costs. In truth we have little idea as to what the relationship is between average and marginal costs in the health care sector. It is unlikely, however, that the situation described above, of constant returns to scale, exists universally and that average costs do indeed equal marginal costs. If this is the case economic efficiency is not (being) attained through an average cost pricing structure.

Ignoring the relationship between average and marginal costs, short run average cost pricing could be advocated for the simple reason that providers are expected to cover their costs, including a fair return on capital. Prices must therefore be set to allow the provider to break even. In the internal market, prices are set, generally, at the level of short run average costs plus a 6 per cent rate of return on capital assets. This restricts the financial surplus a provider can achieve to a regulated 'fair' return on capital. Such pricing, however, limits competition as there is no incentive to do more than cover costs.

Nonetheless providers may face withdrawal from the internal market as a result of making losses through getting their prices wrong or because their costs of production are too high to attract purchasers. Both aspects are important. To get prices right, providers have to know the average cost of producing a case or a hospital day or a bundle of episodes or whatever unit is used to define output. Given the complexities and idiosyncrasies of the production of health care, it is unlikely that this knowledge is readily available. Instead proxies are used which may be accurate or not. These calculated average costs of production may drive purchasers away if the costs of production are higher than those of an alternative provider. Yet use of average costs to encourage competition is meaningful only if comparisons of hospitals take into account their service (and presumably output) mix – i.e. if some yardstick is put in place.

Of course, even with yardstick comparison, the average costs of certain providers may be considered too high by purchasers. Note, however, that average cost is merely total cost divided by total output, however defined. If total cost does not increase, which is likely in a budget constrained system, and total output increases, as it has done in the NHS in recent years, then average cost can only decrease. Average cost can fall then if output increases with no impact on overall expenditure. This might lead to increased pressure on the way capacity is utilised. For example, there may be moves to decrease lengths of stay and substitute day care and out-patient care for expensive in-patient care. Thus, an emphasis on pricing through short-run average costs may lead to short-run cost minimisation relatively quickly, but it is not necessarily consistent with the expansion of capacity.

The optimal level of capacity relates to long term decisions of the potential growth facing any particular provider. To invest in additional capacity, however, the providers must have access to capital funds. Under the old regime funds were controlled centrally. Within the internal market to aid expansion of capacity the Private Funding Initiative was established, where Trust hospitals could circumvent the financial constraints on capital funds within the public sector by raising capital on the private market. The return on capital for a Trust is regulated to be 6 per cent on average, where the average relates to capital interest repayment and public dividend payments if the capital is borrowed within the public sector. If capital monies are raised in the private sector Trusts were still regulated, through their prices, to earn a 6 per cent rate of return on capital. If the private market interest rates were above 6 per cent, Trusts could still borrow privately to fund capital projects through using previous surplus, for example gained through private health care provision, or could be subsidised through the government reducing the public dividend payment. Indeed this implicit subsidy was used extensively in 1993/4 when no public dividend payments were issued for Trust hospitals. While the Private Finance Initiative operated relatively well for small capital schemes – in essence the public dividend subsidy was effective enough for small schemes – as the demand for private capital grew in order to finance major developments like new hospitals, the private banks have sought underwriting guarantees from the government to cover the financial risks of Trusts failing. At this time of writing, this guarantee has not been forthcoming and the initiative is now under threat, in turn threatening to halt all new major capital developments in the NHS.

If short run average cost is falling merely because of output expansion, rather than competition, sooner or later capacity constraints will be met. A demand for new capacity will arise, but if new capital funds are not forthcoming output will face physical constraints and, eventually, short run average costs will rise reflecting diminishing returns to factors of production. Competition may induce the desire to expand output in the short run, after all even in a budget-constrained system it is desirable to have patients if patients generate income. Such competitive forces cannot be sustained in the long run, not least if capital is constrained.

There are other good economic reasons for expecting market competition to be limited under the existing conditions of the internal market. Information on the form of provision being offered may be weak. Indeed, if there is incomplete information on provider quality then prices may act in a perverse manner to signal quality levels – higher average costs could be taken to represent higher quality. Better quality peaches are normally depicted by, all other things being equal, higher prices (although to complicate matters further some peaches turn out to be lemons!). If there is some rapport between purchasers and providers, in that there is a history of dealing with known characteristics of service provision, it may be that there is a reluctance to switch to a new provider (I may suspect that there is little difference in quality between my instant coffee and others, but I know what I get with my brand and I'm sticking to it). Alternatively, in a supply constrained system the purchaser may wish to foster long term relationships to attempt to assure access to provider facilities when demand occurs.

And, of course, there are the political objectives which may mean financial constraints are not completely binding.

Under such circumstances, it would not be surprising to find pre-production negotiations to clarify what the average price relates to – what is it that is being bought at the specified price? This appears to be the area of most dispute in the health care sector (see Hughes in this edition). In some markets such negotiation is implausible. Producers of cars, for example, find it impractical to negotiate with prospective buyers before production takes place. Greater reliance is placed on production for the market as a whole, such that output is disposed of at prices determined when the cars confront demand in the market place. Competition is maintained as the commodity can be specified in great detail and the implicit contract between the consumer and producer is governed through the operation of the market itself; the consumer can choose amongst a large number of sellers. Ultimately the consumer has recourse to the law if there is any imperfection in the exchange. In other words, market exchange is underwritten by the competitive process itself and by the law governing exchange.

With health care it is reasonable to enter into pre-production negotiation to clarify what is being exchanged at what cost. The internal market at this point begins to dissolve into a number of contractual arrangements, each slightly different. For such contracts to have any substantive meaning some means of enforcement must exist. If the competitive nature of the market cannot enforce the contract, then some form of sanction or remedy for breach of contract must be imposed.

The contracts between NHS purchasers and providers do not allow for litigation. There is nevertheless a mechanism for resolving disputes. The Regional Health Authorities act as arbitrators and the Secretary of State for Health will adjudicate in cases where arbitration measures fail. In other words, the enforcement of contracts within the internal market is basically contract specific. The internal market dissolves into a collection of individual contracts rather than a notion of competitive pressure within this type of environment.

In fact, the nature of any damages to be imposed or the precise governance mechanisms that operate within the NHS internal market have not been fully explained. Damages are discussed in terms of remedies 'linked to the degree of actual damage a party is likely to suffer from the other's non-performance', and also in terms of substitute performance

– a provider which cannot fully carry out the terms of its contract should 'subcontract with another facility to do so at its own expense' (HMSO, 1990, p. 31). However, these statements are only suggestions for inclusion in relevant contracts. In other words, it is proposed that the parties should decide for themselves what particular remedy should be imposed for performance failures. So the remedy for breach of contract is formulated in terms of the individual contractual agreement between parties.

All of which suggests that there is not so much a single internal market as a large number of individual contractual agreements between purchasers and providers who have established, or already have, long term relationships with one another and it is these relationships which formalise exchange. Each contract may be different from all others and the underlying governance of the contract may also be peculiar to the particular contract under consideration. Adjudication does not rely on precedence for rulings, but is based on the specifics of individual agreements. In this respect calls for a regulator would seem misplaced as generally regulators focus on sectors rather than individual contractual agreements. Instead, the present system of arbitration could be adequate to govern what are essentially bilateral agreements. Whether providers actually compete with each other or not is a different question and one which turns on the number of alternative suppliers available.

The influence of the contractual environment on the behaviour of the purchasers and providers

How do these contracts affect the behaviour of the organisations, and what is the impact of this contractual environment on the Trusts and GP fund-holders? From the above we may think of the NHS contracts as formalising long term relationships using prospective incentive payment mechanisms to guarantee delivery, at least in most cases. There will also be a competitive fringe operating around these long term relationships. This is formed by the GP fund-holders. While overall the NHS has seen little increase in its real budget since the reforms, these fund-holders hold the prospect of additional revenue for each individual Trust hospital. Even Trusts in stable relationships with local District Health Authority purchasers may compete to secure this additional revenue. It is for this reason that GP fund-holders have become so crucial to the operation of the system.

Nonetheless we might expect long-term relationships, formalised through the use of block contracts, to be formed amongst the main players in this internal market. The block contract offers the lowest powered incentive and is independent of the actual costs incurred. Although, at least in the case of the more typical complex block contracts, it does provide some inducement towards efficient provider behaviour through linking the payment to case mix. Payment begins to become exogenous to provider decisions, at least to the extent that Trusts are unable to reclassify diagnosis decisions or shift costs onto other providers, for example through earlier than optimal discharge of in-patients to rehabilitation hospitals or home.

There is little prior evidence relating to the impact that block contracts may have on provider behaviour, but evidence from the USA on cost and volume type contracts shows a clear relationship between payment in this form and a reduction in output levels. Diagnosis related groups (DRG) based payment systems are a particular example of these prospective cost and volume payment schemes. While it is difficult to specify the optimal quantity of care, evidence does show that prospective payment systems do provide incentives to constrain demand. Sloan, Morrisey and Valvona (1988) show that in the three years prior to the introduction of a prospective payment scheme under Medicare the rate of growth in chest x-rays was stationary, while in the two years after the introduction of the scheme the rate of growth fell by 8 per cent. A number of studies have shown that the introduction of disease contingent prospective payment schemes have led to hospital length of stay falling in a range between 3 per cent and 24 per cent, with consequent impact on costs (Gutterman and Dobson, 1986; Rosko and Broyles, 1987; Fitzgerald *et al.*, 1987; Sloan *et al.*, 1990; Khan *et al.*, 1990). Weisbrod (1991) goes further, indicating that the move to disease contingent prospective payments will curtail the growth in hospital technology. Although again he is careful to point out that, given the difficulties in specifying optimal care, this is not necessarily always associated with welfare improvement. The problem is that it is difficult to identify, observe and verify that the most efficient level of production has taken place. Providers may, therefore, trade quality/quantity of care against cost. Nonetheless what is clear is that payment contracts do affect provider behaviour.

While there is little evidence on the influence of block contracts *per se* on the behaviour of purchasers and providers there is a growing literature which provides some empirical evidence on the operation of the internal market. Csaba and Fenn (1994), noting the predominance of block contracting, tested the hypotheses that this could be explained by purchasers wishing to secure supply of provider service provision. They used data from 71 NHS Hospital Trusts in relation to the proportion of their contractual revenue which is volume-related and that which is fixed. The data for the study were drawn from a report provided by the NHS Management Executive (NHSME) on the income of 157 NHS Trusts in the financial year 1992/3. Hospital revenue was classified into different income categories relating to the nature of the contract with purchasers: the block element; the variable (case-related) element; extra-contractual referral (ECR) revenue; other – mainly private – activity related income; and income generated from sources other than patient services.

The results of this study tended to confirm that block contracts were more likely when there were capacity constraints. In particular, they showed that there is a positive link between the proportion of fixed revenue contracts and the scarcity of provider capacity. Although the block contract still predominates, there was, however, evidence that purchasers are responding to competitive opportunities by negotiating more flexible arrangements where there are clear advantages to do so.

Early work on the impact that assumed competition in the internal market was patchy and suffered from lack of data which, in turn, limited the statistical power of the evidence and the ability to control for important factors (for example case-mix). Even so, this limited evidence did suggest that where management structures were independent of the NHS administration, unit costs were lower. Bartlett and Le Grand (1992) in an early study concluded that Trust hospitals had significantly lower costs than non-Trust hospitals. They noted that this could be a self-selection issue, that is it was the more efficient hospitals which applied for Trust status, rather than the impact of the internal market.

Propper (1994) analysed ECR prices and related costs in four specialities to consider the impact on prices and price–cost mark ups that the cost, market size, bargaining power and a number of hospital and cost characteristics had. Generally, she found that ECR prices were not solely related to costs and that there was weak evidence that market conditions had the expected impacts on price; that is that the stronger the implied competition and the weaker the bargaining power, the lower the price.

The most extensive work, and the only studies to control for case mix so far, on the impact of the internal market on NHS Trusts has been undertaken by Csaba (1995) and Sonderlund *et al.* (1996). Csaba tested a number of hypotheses concerning the determination of average costs of over 200 provider units over three financial years. The explanatory variables included measures of output based on finished consultant episodes, case mix, technology, factor input prices and a number of market structure control variables. Generally the findings were mixed. The higher the concentration of purchaser power in the internal market the lower was provider unit cost, implying that purchasers can influence the efficiency of provider units. There was weak support consistent with the competitive behaviour of provider units being linked to market structure – i.e. the more competitive the structure the lower the unit cost. This is in accordance with the results of the work by Soderlund *et al.* (1996), who found that the considerable variation in hospital costs could be explained through the variation in outputs produced and wage and property costs. They also found that trust status and increased purchaser power were associated with lower hospital costs, although hospital market share had no impact on cost. Csaba (1997), in a different specification, found some support for the hypothesis that competition did lower costs, however.

There has been some research on GP fund-holding also. It has been difficult to evaluate the success of GP fund-holding: there are no formal monitoring structures and the GP fund-holding schemes were introduced along with a number of other changes in primary care, for example changes in the GP contract. Nonetheless the work by Glennerster *et al.*, (1994) suggests that GP fund-holding has led to more efficient practices than those in non-GP fund-holders. Fund-holders have managed, for example, to keep prescription costs down. In 1992/3 the national prescription budget increased by 12 per cent, while for fund-holders the increase was only 8 per cent. Fund-holders tended to have better information and, according to a survey, expressed stronger motivation to improve service delivery. Against such improvements there has been a fear that GP fund-holders refer fewer patients to hospital in an attempt to reduce costs. However, a study by Coulter and Bradlow (1993) found no evidence that this was the case. Baines and Whynes (1996) assessed whether any presumed efficiency displayed by fund-holders could be as a result of self-selection. They found that this could indeed be the case as fund-holding practices were more likely to accord with a number of quality criteria defined by the government and relating to characteristics such as cost control on prescribing and the attainment of service targets, for example with regard to cervical screening. The evidence regarding efficiency gains stemming from GP fund-holders is, therefore, imprecise, and it is not clear whether such gains merely reflect the fact that fund-holding, at least in the early stages, attracted the more efficient practices. At the time of writing, the Audit Commission (1996) had just published a report which found that some £200m of efficiency gains had been more than offset by the costs of running the GP fund-holding scheme. The Commission also pointed out that the overall net benefit of the scheme depended on the evaluation of quality of service benefits, that these did exist but that there was scope for their adoption more widely. As one is so often reduced to concluding, the jury is still out.

CONCLUSIONS ON THE UK REFORMS

Publicly financed competition, as implemented in the British NHS, brings with it a new set of incentives and disincentives. Whether it will succeed in increasing efficiency and consumer sensitivity remains to be seen. Assessment of how purchasing authorities decide which contracts to place, whether contract specifications encourage cost-effective treatment technologies, whether changed incentives to GPs lead to more consumer involvement and whether there are system-wide effects on access and equity in health care, are all important to the evaluation of the efficiency impacts of the reforms. There is little available evaluative evidence on any of these aspects. At present it is not clear that the contracting underlying this competitive structure will be adequately specified to cover all the difficulties associated with quality and outcome uncertainties associated with this sector. If contracts cannot be adequately specified a number of responses may evolve. Given that the budgets will be prospective there are clear incentives to curtail expenditure by providing average, rather than high quality care, even under capitation systems. There is also considerable scope for dispute, the resolution of which depends upon the precise nature of the governance structure. This is currently far from precise. Given such uncertainties, the inherently incomplete nature of contract specification and the risk aversion of the major players, it is likely that long-term relationships between players will evolve as a means of attenuating the uncertainties underlying the contracting process. If this does occur then the presumed benefits arising from regulated competition will be somewhat diminished. Given the costs and benefits of the system it is certainly not the case that there are clear efficiency advantages to be achieved. Whether these evolve remains a question for debate. In this context it is perhaps not surprising that the internal market appears to be evolving into a multiplicity of long term and long-standing relationships. If competitive pressures are weak, then the impact of the new contractual arrangements will be seen through the new behavioural relationships that evolve through the splitting of purchasers and providers. The continuing predominance of the block contract suggests that the contracting parties remain unwilling to embrace the much-heralded benefits of more specific exchange mechanisms and are hedging their bets against all the uncertainties which have accompanied the change in the organisational structure of the NHS. The efficiency of the internal market can only be judged through a better understanding of the organisational environment within which it operates. It is this enviornment that the following papers discuss.

References

Appleby, J. *et al.* (1994) 'Monitoring managed competion', in: Robinson, R. and J. Le Grand (ed.) *Evaluating the NHS reform* (London: King's Fund Institute).

Audit Commission (1996) *What the Doctor Ordered: A study of GP Fundholders in England and Waler* (London: HMSO).

Baines, D. and D. Whynes (1996) 'Selection bias in fundholding', *Health Economics*, 5, 129–40.

Bartlett, W. and J. Le Grand (1992) *The Impact of the NHS Reforms on Hospital Costs: Some Preliminary Findings* (SAUS Discussion Paper, University of Bristol).

Coulter, A. and J. Bradlow (1993) 'Effect of the NHS reforms on general practitioner's referral patterns', *British Medical Journal*, 306, 433–7.

Crump, B., Cubbon, B., Drummond, M., Hawkes, R., and Marchmant, M. (1991) Fundholding in general practice and financial risk, *British Medical Journal*, 302, 1582–84.

Csaba, I. (1995) *Hospital Costs and the regulated health market: An empirical analysis of the British health reforms* (Paper presented at the 4th European Health Economics Association, Stockholm).

Csaba, I. (1997) 'Hospital costs, organisational slack and quasi-markets', paper presented to the Health Economics Study Group, Liverpool.

Csaba, I. and P. Fenn (1994) 'Contractual Choice in the Managed Health Care Market – An Economic Model and Empirical Analysis' (Discussion Paper 94.2, Oxford Centre for Health Economics Research).

Fenn, P., Rickman N., and McGuire, A. (1994) 'Contracts, supply assurance and the delivery of health care', *Journal of Health Economics*, 13, 1–20.

Fitzgerald, J., L. Fagan, W. Tierney, and R. Dittus (1987) 'Changing patterns of hip fracture care before and after implementation of the prospective payment system', *Journal of the American Medical Association*, 258, 218–21.

Gutterman, S. and A. Dobson (1986) 'Impact of the Medicare prospective payment system for hospitals', *Health Care Financing Review*, 7, 97–114.

Glennerster, H., M. Matsaganis, P. Owen, and S. Hancock (1994) 'GP fundholding: wild card or winning hand?', in Robinson, R. and J. Le Grand (eds) *Evaluating the NHS Reforms* (London: King's Fund Institute).

HMSO (1983) 'The Management Enquiry' *The Griffiths Report* (London: HMSO).

HMSO (1990) 'Funding and Contracts for Hospital Services', *NHS Review Working Paper* (2) (London: HMSO).

Khan, K., E. Keeler, M. Sherwood, D. Rogers, D. Draper *et al.* (1990) 'Comparing outcomes of care before and after implementation of the DRG prospective payment system', *Journal of the American Medical Association*, 264, 1984–88.

McGuire, A., P. Fenn and K. Mayhew (eds) (1991) *Providing Health Care* (Oxford: OUP).

Propper, C. (1994) *Market structure and prices: the responses of hospitals in the UK NHS to competition* (University of Bristol Discussion Paper, Nov. 1994).

Quam, L. (1991) 'Post war American health care: the many costs of market failure', in McGuire *et al.* (eds) *Providing Health Care* (Oxford: OUP).

Rosho, M.D. and Broyles, R.W. (1987) 'Short-term responses of hospitals to DRG prospective pricing mechanisms in New Jersey', *Medical Care*, 25, 88–99.

Sloan, F., M. Morrisey and J. Valvona (1988) 'Medicare prospective payment and the use of medical technologies in hospitals' *Medical Care*, 26, 837–53.

Soderlund, N., I. Csaba, A. Gray, R. Milne, and J. Raftery (1996) *The Impact of the British reforms on hospital efficiency – an analysis of the first three years* (Discussion paper, Department of Public Medicine, University of Oxford).

Weisbrod, B. (1991) 'The health care quadrilemma: an essay on technological change, insurance, quality of care and cost containment', *Journal of Economic Literature*, 24, 523–52.

2 The New NHS in a Global Context: is it taking us where we want to be?[1]

Cam Donaldson and Gavin Mooney

SUMMARY

In this paper, the new NHS is put in a global context, comparing the UK internal market arrangements with changes occurring in other health care systems. An assessment is made of whether the new UK NHS will result in more efficient and equitable health care provision than the 'old' NHS. Regarding financing of health care, most countries seem to be moving in the direction of NHS or public-insurance-based systems. New Zealand and The Netherlands are among the few countries attempting to inject competition into health care financing. There is a greater move, globally, towards competition in the provision of services. In terms of allocative efficiency and equity, we believe that, on balance, the new NHS will bring no improvement. Indeed, in terms of equity, it may be detrimental. If there is any improvement, it is likely to be in technical efficiency.

INTRODUCTION

In considering and appraising the new NHS as outlined by the editors in their introduction, this paper attempts to put the changes into a broad perspective, especially, but not solely, in the context of change in health care systems in other countries. How substantial are the changes in the UK? Are other health services moving in the same or different directions? What criteria of success should be applied, and how successful are the changes likely to be?

In sections 2–4 of this paper, we examine the move to the NHS in the context of financing and then in terms of provision, drawing on

17

experiences from other countries. The experiences we refer to are largely, but not solely, those of countries which have recently changed (or which have outlined proposals for change) to more competitive systems of finance and provision. In the fifth section, the new NHS as compared with the old is appraised.

The performance criteria adopted are as follows:

(i) allocative efficiency (i.e., trying to ensure that resources are spent where they can do most good);
(ii) productive efficiency, in the sense of ensuring that chosen objectives get met at least cost;
(iii) equity, which is concerned with fairness of distribution in health care, most frequently expressed as equal access for equal need.

REFORMS IN FINANCING AND PROVISION

It is possible to have a market in health care provision (e.g., competition between hospitals) without a market in finance (e.g., competition between insurers), and vice versa. It is erroneous to suppose that one must necessarily accompany the other. The aim of the UK reforms is to retain the advantages of a tax-based system in combination with the advantages of a market in provision. The possible mix of competition in

FINANCE

	Competitive	Non-competitive
Competitive	*(1)*	*(2)*
	New Zealand	*UK*
	The Netherlands	*California*
	HMOs	*Medicaid*
		Leningrad
PROVISION		
	(4)	*(3)*
		Italy
		Spain
Non-competitive		*Denmark*
		Eastern Europe

Figure 2.1

finance and provision is displayed in Figure 2.1. The UK system has no competition in finance but does have competition in provision. Thus, it sits mainly in quadrant 2.

REFORMS IN FINANCING HEALTH CARE

The main possible reforms on the financing side are at the system level. They relate to how funds are raised. The primary options are:

(i) taxation;
(ii) public/social insurance; and
(iii) modified private insurance (including 'Health Maintenance Organisation' (HMO) type systems)[2]

In the purest form, HMOs involve financial intermediaries competing for financial contributions from (potential) customers. In taxation and public insurance systems, no such competition takes place, although attempts have been made to simulate this within mainly-public systems (see the examples of The Netherlands and New Zealand below).

The UK reforms did not focus too much on financing. This is because of the advantages of retaining a tax-based system. These advantages are:

(i) maintenance of universal coverage thus avoiding the consequence of 'adverse selection', which results in a failure to cover adequately high risk/cost cases;
(ii) distributional advantages; and
(iii) low administrative cost.

All of these advantages are likely to be lost when introducing competition in finance. They can be overcome without necessarily resorting to a tax-based system, but other options are often administratively cumbersome. There does not appear to be any compelling reason for switching to these other options (Donaldson and Gerard, 1993).

A tax-based system can be funded from general taxation, a hypothecated tax (i.e., earmarked specifically for health services) or a general public insurance system (which could possibly cover more than health care and with contributions which are not experience-rated).[3]

The Australian health care system provides a good example of a hypo-thecated tax in the form of the Medicare levy. However, it has never been the intention that this levy should cover all of the public sector's health care costs, the majority being met directly from general taxation. There would seem to be no point in the UK moving to an Australian system of health care financing. Costs of change would be incurred for no obvious benefit; likewise with the Australians moving towards an NHS-type system. The method of funding that has evolved in these countries has done so as a result of reasons peculiar to each (Palmer and Short, 1989).

By definition, a system of funding direct from taxation maintains cover for everyone in the population, avoiding the problem of adverse selection. Adverse selection arises in private health care insurance systems and leads to premiums being experience rated.[4] With premiums related to illness experience, it is likely that many higher risk people would not take out insurance as it would be too costly. Compulsory participation, through taxation, ensures that one hundred per cent coverage of the population is achieved.

Competition between financial intermediaries could still take place alongside attempts to remove the problem of adverse selection. The most famous examples of this are the USA Medicare and Medicaid schemes for elderly and poor people respectively. These schemes are financed from a combination of payroll taxes, federal and state taxation, and, in the case of Medicare, premiums paid by elderly people themselves (Ginsburg, 1988). Yet, inevitably, people fall between the cracks. In the USA it has been estimated that, in 1977, 50 million people were inadequately covered against the costs of catastrophic illness and, more recently, that 37 million people (17 per cent of the population) have no cover whatsoever (Farley, 1985; Wilensky, 1988). Recent attempts have been made in The Netherlands and New Zealand to introduce competition in finance whilst retaining 100 per cent coverage. These attempts are described below.

The advantage of a tax-based system in terms of redistribution is that, by detaching premiums from expected risk levels and making them compulsory, wealth is redistributed from those with low *ex ante* expectations of illness to those at high risk. Individuals are effectively charged one form of community rate, which is dependent on ability to pay but not on previous experience of ill health. A progressive tax-financed system has the ability to redistribute according to two indicators of individual well-being: the income of the payer and, at least potentially, the need, for the recipient, of care. It can thus be more efficient than any form of redistribution based on income alone.

Regarding administrative costs, a tax-based system is virtually free of loading problems. Examples of costs associated with private health care insurance are marketing and premium collection. These costs are loaded on to premiums. In this respect, a tax-based system is probably the most efficient way of collecting monies to finance health care (often referred to as 'piggybacking' onto the existing system of tax collection). Recent estimates of the administrative costs of the USA health care system have put it at 22 per cent and rising (Himmelstein and Woolhandler, 1986; Woolhandler and Himmelstein, 1991). It is thought that more competition (through HMOs) has resulted in increased administrative costs of advertising and utilisation review (Evans, 1987; Quam, 1989). Evans (1990) has described the effect of such activities as follows:

> A large and growing share of the American total is spent, not on doctors and nurses, but on accountants, management consultants, and public relations specialists. Their contribution to the health of the American public is difficult to discern (unless one is trained in neoclassical economics and is able to see with the eye of faith).

Referring to data from Australia, it has been claimed that in 1982–3 (the year before the introduction of universal health care insurance) management expenses of private funds amounted to 14.8 per cent of benefits paid to claimants, whilst in its first full year of operation, the corresponding figure for Medicare (Australia's second universal public insurance scheme) was 4.7 per cent (Richardson, 1987). Thus, there appear to be definite diseconomies in competition.

Even some European countries are moving towards NHS-type systems, presumably at least in part because of the administrative costs of running systems financed from social insurance. Spain and Italy are examples of this (Italian Ministry of Justice, 1988; Ministerio de Sanidad y Consumo, 1989).

Prior to the legislation introducing the new NHS, several right-wing policy analysts discussed the possibility of altering the system of financing health care in the UK (Brittan, 1988; Butler and Pirie, 1988;

Letwin and Redwood, 1988). However, this option was not taken up by the Conservative Government which has stressed that:

> the NHS is, and will continue to be, open to all, regardless of income, and financed mainly out of general taxation. (Secretaries of State for Health, Wales, N. Ireland and Scotland, 1989)

From an original position of support for more radical reform, the Government came up with proposals for competition in provision, but not finance. As we have said, this puts the UK in quadrant 2 of Figure 2.1. Some countries, like Denmark, are in quadrant 4, which is where the UK used to be.

There are other countries, however, which have tried to inject an element of competition into the financing of health care. Recent proposals in New Zealand concentrate mainly on provider competition (see next section), but also permit people to opt out of regional health authority cover to a private sector Health Care plan (HCP), taking a weighted financial allocation with them (Dearden, 1991). This element of competition in finance is what primarily distinguishes the New Zealand reforms from those in the UK.

Health care in The Netherlands has a tradition of finance via private insurers. Recent reforms, based on the Dekker/Simons proposals, include a system whereby consumers pay a maximum rate, with Government contributing top-up payments which reflect individuals' risk levels (Van de Ven, 1989). These reforms also concentrate more on provider competition (see next section). This puts New Zealand and The Netherlands in quadrant 1 of Figure 2.1. In these systems, financial intermediaries are attempting to attract consumers' money, although a large element of what the consumer brings with them is from the public purse.

The Dutch reforms do not constitute a major change, given previous reliance on private insurers. Indeed, these reforms have still not been implemented (Sheldon, 1994). However, the New Zealand reforms are perhaps more surprising, given that it was the first country to have a welfare state. Whether the benefits of such competition in finance outweigh the costs remains to be seen. One would suspect, however, that the administrative costs would be great. In addition, it is not clear whether, in New Zealand, those opting for private cover can top up their weighted allocation. If so, and if enough people opt out, a two-tiered system is likely to develop, a system that appears to be an anathema to most people in the UK. Also, such a system could distort priority-setting according to need, with resources going to those who opt out and can afford to pay top-up premiums. However, the change gives the impression of being greater than it actually is. The weighted allocation is still funded from taxation, to which everyone has to contribute. If top-ups are allowed, it is likely that a situation similar to that in the UK will arise: a dominant public sector alongside a small private sector, in terms of both finance and provision. Such questions are obviously of importance to the New Zealand Government, as this part of the New Zealand reforms has yet to be implemented. There remains doubt as to whether it ever will be (Scott, 1995).

Another possible financial reform, sometimes associated with revenue generation and often politely referred to as 'cost recovery', is patient charges. Such charges are most commonly associated with private health care insurance, but can be implemented within any system. There is little doubt that they deter consumption, but there are serious question marks over whether it is 'frivolous consumption' that is deterred, their equity effects and, given the influence of doctors over demand for health care, whether doctors can switch their demand-inducing abilities to those who can afford the charges (Donaldson and Gerard, 1989). If the last effect holds up, the same amount of care would be provided but to less effect, as those who can afford the charges are likely to be *ceteris paribus* those less in need of effective health care.

Charges do not play a significant role in health care financing in the UK. However, the introduction of charges for eye and dental checks in 1989 do represent major changes of policy. Contrary to the above argument on supplier-induced demand, it can be claimed that charges reorientate priorities back towards less healthy and less well-off groups. These groups tend to be exempt from the charges; the group whose demand is affected by charges being better off both financially and in terms of health. This argument is too simplistic. Amongst the non-exempt group, charges may delay or prevent patients from receiving the medication they need (Ryan and Yule, 1993). In another, previously similar, health care system (New Zealand), the intention is that charges will play a more significant role. However, once again the New Zealand reforms have floundered on this aspect, in-patient charges for all groups being abolished in 1993 (Scott, 1995).

In summary, it would seem that the UK Government recognises the advantage of a tax-based system of health care financing. Globally, there has not been that much change in financing either. Certainly, there is little convergence of systems in this regard. Depending on what happens in Eastern Europe, more divergence could occur. Most countries have non-competitive systems of financing, Eastern Europe included (see quadrant 4 of Figure 2.1). In this respect, perhaps there is little room for more convergence. However, the pressure for change in Eastern European countries is great, perhaps even change for change's sake. This could take (indeed, has taken) these countries towards private sources of health care finance. What can be said, however, is that there is more movement, and probably convergence, on the side of provision of health care. It is this to which we now turn.

REFORMS IN PROVISION

The new NHS in the UK has focused more on stimulating competition in provision. The rationale behind provider markets is fairly clear. The aim is to introduce a systematic financial signalling system of the sort that would exist in a well-ordered market. Information on cost and quality should guide purchasers and providers towards allocative and technical efficiency in health care. (Allocative and technical efficiency are each defined more fully in the following section.)

Purchasers (mainly health authorities, but increasingly some fund-holding general practitioners) will decide on health care programmes to which they wish to allocate money on behalf of their patients. The aim is for them to allocate their limited funds to programmes where the pay-off in terms of health gains for money spent is highest. Knowing that purchasers are shopping around should give providers the incentive to offer to produce such health gains at least cost.

The first area of convergence concerns the UK reforms in general practice. Allowing fund-holding practices to purchase a limited range of hospital services reflects the HMO model in the USA. The main difference is that the HMO model involves competition on the financing side, which puts HMOs in quadrant 1 of Figure 2.1 rather than quadrant 2. Likewise, in the Leningrad experiment in Russia, hospital budgets for 37 specialities were transferred to polyclinics on the basis of average cost per case (Hakansson *et al.*, 1988). Polyclinics are the main provider of primary care and are also involved in some specialist out-patient investigation, treatment and rehabilitation. Previously, with polyclinics run on a separate budget, there was an incentive for them to refer patients on to hospital. Experiments such as those in Russia and the UK have been referred to as 'demand-side socialism'; the new NHS concentrates on stimulating competition on the supply side whilst con-sumers, who cannot choose their district health authority or polyclinic, are covered as a result of being resident in a particular catchment area (Culyer, 1991).

Secondly, it is still the intention to implement purchaser–provider arrangements, such as those between health authorities and hospitals, in The Netherlands and New Zealand. The Dekker/Simons reforms in the Dutch system include proposals for insurers to purchase services from suppliers of health and social care on the basis of cost and qual-ity. In New Zealand, four regional health authorities (RHAs) are to be created. They will purchase care on behalf of their population (about 800 000 each) from competitors from public, private and voluntary sec-tors. Progress with implementation of reforms in The Netherlands and New Zealand is, however, unclear. As well as problems mentioned above, the latter has struggled on the definition of 'Core Services' (i.e., that group of services which is to be made available for the whole population) (Mooney and Salmond, 1995).

In all of these countries, including the UK, the private sector (in terms of provision) is not being explicitly encouraged or discouraged. The aim is simply to leave it to the market to decide the fate of such pro-viders. Only the UK has explicitly legislated to allow larger hospitals to get out of health authority control to become independent NHS Hospi-tal Trusts. The aim here is to help ensure competition, allowing Trusts to break away from the bureaucracy of health authority control. How-ever, the proposition is doubtful; given the monopoly position of most providers and the monopsony position of most purchasers, co-opera-tion rather than competition is the more likely scenario. The only geo-graphical area where competition was likely to have a significant effect (London) has effectively been taken out of the internal market, as reflected in the UK Government's recent decision to postpone the cre-ation of Trusts there. At the time of writing, the position of London's hospitals remains under review.

Even in the USA there is an element of internal markets. Introduced in 1982, the California State Medicaid selective contracting scheme permits Medicaid (and now private insurers) to contract selectively with hospitals and other providers of care, the aim being to stimulate price competition among these providers. Previously, this could not be done because of the threat of anti-trust prosecution of funders by providers. The State Medicaid programme and private payers have used the system to negotiate discounts with providers (Melnick and Zwanziger, 1988). This puts the California State Medicaid programme in quadrant 2 of Figure 2.1. With HMOs in quadrant 1, it can be seen that the USA health care system is difficult to characterise in just one quadrant of this figure. It probably has elements in all four quadrants.

In creating a market for health care provision, we can thus see much more convergence of systems than in their financing mechanisms. As one of the first, the global significance of the UK's new NHS is very great.

WHERE DO WE WANT TO BE? AND WILL THE NEW NHS TAKE US THERE?

Here we discuss the extent to which the new NHS is likely to be judged successful, using the criteria set out at the end of the first section. We first distinguish between two forms of efficiency, allocative efficiency and productive efficiency, before going on to consider the effects of the new NHS on each of these as well as on equity.

Allocative and productive efficiency

Resources are scarce. Thus competing objectives cannot all be met in full. Allocative efficiency is concerned with the allocation of scarce resources across those competing objectives ideally in such a way as to maximise the benefit to society from these resources. As such this would normally be seen as being most likely to be achieved by embracing or at least reflecting society's preferences (which are likely to vary from country to country). It would also, in the context of health care, not necessarily be restricted to health services resources but would take account of the impact of health services on the use of other resources, especially those of patients (for example, patient time) in getting to health care facilities.

Productive efficiency relates to how well resources are used to meet some given objective. Consequently, it may be looked on as a lower level form of efficiency where the task is to find low cost – indeed, ideally least cost – solutions to meeting given goals.

In summary, if somewhat crudely, allocative efficiency is about which objectives to choose to meet and to what extent; productive efficiency is about how to meet these objectives.

Allocative efficiency

With respect to allocative efficiency, it could be argued that the old NHS did not adequately reflect social preferences with respect to certain types of problems and patients – for example, people with mental illness and elderly people. Services for these patients were often referred to as Cinderella services. However, whether the apparently low priority given to these groups was in reality a result of some misrepresentation or ignoring of social preferences with respect to their care is open to debate. It may reflect some preferences by individuals for 'high tech', acute medicine which more readily catches the imagination of the public.

Again, in the old NHS there were relatively few incentives beyond professional standards and the ethics of delivery of high quality care, for adequate account to be taken of the impact of different policy choices in the health care sector on resources outside the NHS budget. This was particularly true with respect to costs falling on patients, with often seemingly low or zero values placed on patient time. Also, there was little incentive to take into account various costs falling on local authority services such as the home help service, housing, etc.

Will the new NHS fair better on allocative efficiency both with respect to reflecting social preferences and in taking account of a wider use of resources than just those within the NHS budget?

Overall the judgement at this stage of the development of the NHS is mixed. First, through increased emphasis on the consumer in the reformed NHS, it is intended that consumers' preferences and thereby social preferences will have more influence on how resources are deployed than in the past. However, at this level the reforms emphasise the consumer as an individual patient rather than as patients collectively. Yet, given the nature of the commodity health care, consumers' preferences at this individual level are unlikely to make much impact on allocative efficiency. As currently conceived, therefore, the extent to which increased collective consumer choice will affect allocative efficiency will be small, although when it does occur it will be positive. However, the suggestion that the exercises on needs assessment and priority setting in purchasing should be informed by community values may represent an attempt to increase the influence of consumers collectively (NHS Management Executive, 1992). How this will be achieved remains, in our view, problematical.

A further relevant and more fundamental point, however, is that there is a belief that in the new NHS individual consumers' preferences ought to be the basis of social preferences. This view is open to challenge. Indeed there can be a conflict between what is 'good' on the basis of individual patient choice and what is deemed socially 'good'. Given the nature of the commodity health care and, in particular, the consumer's imperfections of knowledge of the commodity and in turn his or her dependence on the doctor as an agent, we would seriously question whether the consumerism built into the new NHS is the way to reflect social preferences. It may be that consumers themselves would recognise their own deficiencies in expressing their preferences and instead settle for an agency relationship here, i.e. with expert policy makers exercising preferences on behalf of society.

Second, the split of purchaser and provider and the responsibility placed on the purchasers to meet the needs of their population seem capable of improving allocative efficiency. Purely from the viewpoint of meeting needs there is no *a priori* reason why the apparently medical-profession-led preferences for the acute sector, especially in hospital medicine, should continue. If this does occur then elderly and mentally ill people would perhaps move to a more equal footing with other client groups.

However, for this argument to stand up, purchasers will need to behave differently from the health authorities of the past. The principle of addressing the needs of their population has not in fact changed. Consequently, the issue here is dependent on whether purchasers will react differently as a result of having to face the very explicit choice of: what services should we buy? We would judge that this increased explicitness may have a small but positive effect on allocative efficiency in getting greater awareness of the choices to be made between different groups who are in competition for the resources available.

As pointed out above, one of the key advantages of the old NHS *vis-à-vis* many other forms of health care systems was that it provided access to care for all. There were no system-induced problems of adverse selection or of cream skimming which led to some people having experience-rated private insurance, others (who are old or poor) receiving public cover (as in the USA) and others (who cannot afford private cover and are not poor enough or old enough to receive public cover) falling between the cracks.

An alternative is simply to have compulsory cover with some form of payment system which might also be compulsory but not necessarily linked to risk. In essence this latter type of cover is what the old and the new NHS provide. The problem with this system is that, even if it is allocatively efficient, some people still fall between the cracks because not all need can be met with available resources. In comparing the new with the old, the key questions are whether the new cracks are different from the old and, if so, whether they are indicative of more or less allocative efficiency.

Improved allocative efficiency will result in the bad buys, from a social perspective, losing out rather than the bad risks. Bad buys are those for whom, with limited health care resources, it is socially justified not to spend on them; bad risks are those who are expensive to the insurer. Avoiding bad buys means spending in such a way that the health of the community is as high as it can be. Avoiding bad risks means keeping spending down without regard to health. The two are not necessarily the same.

On this issue, so much will depend on how the purchaser–provider split works in practise. If it pushes the new NHS in the direction of improved allocative efficiency, then clearly this is welcome; if in the direction of introducing cream skimming then this is more worrying. An overall judgement must await more empirical evidence.

Another aspect of the reforms which can affect allocative efficiency is GP budgets. While there are potential advantages of such budgets, they also represent a very real way of introducing cream skimming (Matsaganis and Glennerster, 1994). Potentially, GP budget-holders have a clear incentive to avoid expensive patients and/or to minimise the amount of time they spend with them. From a financial point of view, *ceteris paribus*, any GP budget-holder will prefer a population of young males than an elderly one or one with many women of child-bearing age. But of course much will depend on how the budget is set. Indeed in this context, this seems to be the crucial consideration with respect to allocative efficiency, especially for those bad risk but good buy groups among those previously served only by the Cinderella services in the old NHS. In the context of prescribing budgets, it is not possible to determine efficiency without information on the benefits of different preparations (Healey *et al.*, 1994). Our judgement would be that, as currently constructed, GP budgets are unlikely to promote allocative efficiency.

At another level, the reforms may well help to promote allocative efficiency. There will, in future, be far more concern about where the money is going than there has been in the past. (This is built into the reforms as one of the central planks of it, i.e. the idea of money following the patients.) Costs and costing will undoubtedly be more visible as a result of both the purchaser–provider split and GP fund-holding. Thus, while allocative efficiency is driven by social preferences, it is anchored in resource limitations. The reforms will clearly emphasise, and make more explicit, the scarcity of the resources available.

As indicated above, allocative efficiency ideally looks at the allocation of health care resources whether or not the resources fall within the NHS budget. There has to be some concern that the tendency which existed in the old NHS to allow health service resource use to dominate the cost side of decision makers' thinking will be heightened still further by the reforms rather than reduced. This is manifested in the concept of 'business plans' introduced in the new NHS which inevitably emphasise costs, especially those financial costs falling on the NHS. *Inter alia*, this may increase the already developing tendency to 'offload' elderly patients to the social services. The effect may be small – taking account of non-NHS costs has never been a particular strength of the NHS (although the advent of 'option appraisal' of capital developments in the early 1980s did encourage a wider view of costs). Overall, however, we see the new NHS in this context being a definite, even if small, minus.

Productive efficiency

It is here that the new NHS is more likely to be successful. Given the Government's concern with market forces in the economy as a whole and its campaign for increased privatisation in the 1980s, the basic ideological drive for NHS reform arose from the view that market forces were more likely to promote greater productive efficiency than did the old style NHS. There were no strong views in the Government that the level of spending was widely wrong; there were no major governmental concerns about a need to reallocate resources across different groups of clients; and equity appears not to have been much in evidence at all in the move to reform.

In the context of productive efficiency, the key elements appear to be the resource management initiative, the purchaser–provider split, medical audit, and GP budgeting. Each is examined here briefly from the point of view of how it might be expected to contribute to greater technical efficiency.

In combination, there are grounds for believing that the new NHS will go some way to improving productive efficiency. The resource management initiative (although not strictly part of the reforms package) could, if implemented properly, bring a greater awareness of resource constraints and thereby the concept of opportunity cost to the forefront of clinical decision making. It is clinical decision making that holds the key to productive efficiency and it will not be achieved unless clinicians are forced, as resource management can do, to appreciate the need to aim to minimise their resource use in pursuing their clinical goals. Much depends on the extent to which the previously more disparate aims of clinicians and hospital managers become more integrated under the new arrangements (Farrar, 1993).

The purchaser–provider split again helps to bring to the fore the need for delivering productive efficiency. Here, however, it can only be where the internal market does work, in the sense of there being various competing units, that we can expect improved productive efficiency actually to be delivered, or at least costs held down below what they otherwise might have been. Normally, in situations of monopoly (of which there will be many outside cities), costs would be expected to rise; but this should be tempered by the presence of monopsony purchasers (health authorities). In these cases, not much change can be expected; purchasers and providers will have to co-operate, much as they did in the old NHS.

Where productive efficiency may come to grief, however, is with respect to quality, or, as we would prefer to call it, effectiveness. The pressure to keep costs down may turn out to be real but the pressure to keep effectiveness up may not be. Furthermore, there may be some pressure for quality competition whereby hospitals obtain high-technology but ineffective equipment just to look good. Competitors may feel the need to do the same or they may otherwise lose out on revenue. Such competition will hamper not only productive efficiency but also allocative efficiency.

Medical audit clearly has a very considerable role to play here. However, the evidence to date suggests cause for concern on this front on two points. First, the current emphasis of audit lies in getting doctors (and only doctors) to agree about what they think is good medical practice. This will almost certainly involve setting standards that are too expensive to achieve. Such a form of audit must embrace from the beginning not just effective care but productively efficient care. There is little evidence to suggest that this approach to audit will be embraced (Hopkins, 1992).

Second, the current audit movement is based on the idea that if clinicians know that a particular form of practice has been deemed good then they will adopt that practice. Such an idea is not new; it has already failed elsewhere. There is thus a need to consider what package of incentives should accompany any guidelines on audit to get clinicians to change their behaviour.

Finally, there is the impact of the new NHS on productive efficiency in general practice. Here we think that the reforms will improve produtive efficiency. GP fund-holders do have some real incentives to keep costs down and to refer more rationally. Additionally they may have at least some motivation to keep quality up as a result of increased choice for patients in deciding on their GP and the resultant increased competition between GPs. The idea of the GP budget, even if it is seldom expressed in this form, is based on the notion of the GP as the patient's agent trying to buy the most efficient care for his/her patients. That is welcome.

In summary, it is clinical decision making which in the end will determine the productive efficiency of any health care system. That means that doctors have to change their behaviour and become more aware of both the costs and the benefits of what they are doing. The audit movement is central and its current focus does not encourage optimism that technical efficiency will be greatly improved in the NHS. However, resource management and the purchaser–provider split *working together*, leaves some cause for optimism in this regard.

Equity

We believe that equity ought to be one of the performance indicators for any health service. However, it figures little in the new NHS. The new NHS was never intended to promote greater equity and there seems little doubt that it will not.

Here, of course, we need to guard against leaving the impression that the old NHS was highly successful on this front. Certainly, equality of access has been one of the cornerstones of the NHS and has been promoted through keeping patient payments on the whole restricted to few services.

Again, the RAWP formula which allocated resources from the centre to the regions was in principle based on equality of access. However, the reality on equity as a whole fell short of the promise even in the old NHS.

But even accepting this, the new NHS is likely to represent a backward step with respect to equity. For example one of the side effects of GP fund-holding is that patients from practices which are fund-holding (covering about one half of the populations of England and Scotland respectively) may get priority in hospital treatment ahead of other patients. This is precisely because hospitals may be prepared to try to attract the GP fund-holders. Contracts with them are clearly appealing to hospitals and deals have been struck with them to give GP fund-holding practices special priority in having their patients treated – this gives rise to a new form of inequity in the NHS. (At the time of writing, GP fund-holding has been extended to smaller practices, it seems, at least in part, as a result of concerns for the inequities introduced through fund-holding. However, as GP fund-holding increases, the ability of the system to continue giving all fund-holding practices priority must be questioned.)

How geographical equity will change is unclear. While RAWP is changing, it appears not to be changing radically. At the time of writing, there are signs that the Government may be setting out to protect the overbedded and generally over-resourced (in RAWP terms at least) London and the South East. Otherwise, the new NHS might well have exposed and removed at least some of this over-provision, proving that the capital is over-resourced. The internal market, as we have tried to indicate earlier, is likely to work best where there is high density population and a lot of hospitals in the market. London clearly best fits that description in the UK. Yet, there are signs that market forces will not be allowed to have their say in precisely the place where they might work best (Shackley and Healey, 1993).

CONCLUSIONS

It seems that competition in finance has been rejected as a policy option by the UK Government and not without good reason. The current system of raising funds is cheap, provides 100 per cent coverage of the population and seems to provide some distributional advantages.

Competition in health care provision was settled upon, perhaps as an ideological compromise. Nevertheless, this type of innovation already existed in some parts of the world and will be introduced in more over the coming years. The global significance of the UK's new NHS is, therefore, considerable.

In areas of high concentration of facilities (as in London), one would expect greater productive efficiency as competitors seek to keep costs down. However, the process of competition in London has been halted, at least temporarily.

Competition in quality is possible, but unlikely. Hospitals may purchase ineffective diagnostic equipment to look good. Other competitors may feel compelled to do the same in case they lose out on revenue. It is the hope that this sort of behaviour would be mitigated through contracts between purchasers and providers. But, if not, it would lead to less productive efficiency and less allocative efficiency (in a cash-limited system, the resources would have to come from some other activity to pay for increased, but useless, 'quality'). Negative effects on quality could also occur. Perhaps these are easier to picture. It will be interesting to observe which of these effects prevails.

Where there is not much competition, monopoly providers will exist. On its own, this situation would lead to inefficiencies. However, the dominant position of monopolies should be tempered by the existence of monopsony purchasers of services (i.e., health authorities). In such situations, not much change is expected – providers and purchasers will have to get on with each other, much as they did in the old NHS.

One main difference here will be that the whole system will (it is hoped) be fed by more information on costs and outcome, leading to more rational decisions about what to buy (allocative efficiency) and to reduced costs (where possible) of what is bought (productive efficiency). This should increase the probability of maximisation of health gains for resources spent.

It is important to bear in mind that, in a cash-limited system, provision of more information will have opportunity costs. Little is known about these. It could be, however, that waiting times for operations are not reduced to the extent that they otherwise would have been (they may indeed increase), as a result of money being diverted from elective surgery to finance more managers. A judgement is required as to what level of information is optimal.

The role of the consumer in guiding the system will be limited. More account will be taken of consumer views, but it is difficult to see a way in for consumers as major decision makers regarding the allocation of resources in the new NHS.

In monitoring progress on these issues, experience from the UK and around the world over the coming decade will be of crucial importance. In this regard, our assessment is merely a starting point.

Notes

1. This chapter is an edited version of an earlier paper with the same title which appeared in *Health Policy*, 25 (parts 1 and 2), 1993, 9–24.
2. Health maintenance organisations (HMOs) have evolved over the last decade in the USA as a means of stimulating more genuine competition in the USA health care market. HMOs provide (or arrange and pay for) comprehensive health care for a fixed periodic payment (or premium) per capita, or per family. Consumers pay a fixed proportion of the premium, usually with a subsidy from employers or social security. This gives consumers an incentive to shop around when the time comes for renewal. The premium is set in advance and is independent of the volume of services provided to the individual during the period of cover. This gives the provider an incentive to be cost conscious.
3. Experience-rated premiums for insurance reflect an individual's (or family's) experience of health. Those with a worse track record pay higher premiums. Paradoxically in health care this would mean that rich people would on average pay less than poor people because they also tend to be healthier than poor people.
4. In a competitive market, if an insurance company has no idea of risk status it will set a premium which reflects the average risk level of the community. This is community rating. However, for those in the community who perceive themselves to be at low risk, this premium will be too high. They may drop out of insurance. This, in turn, will force up the average risk level of those remaining insured. Premiums will rise and another group of relatively healthy people may drop out because, again, premiums are too high. This is adverse selection. In a competitive system, the presence of a low-risk, uninsured group gives insurance companies the chance to tailor premiums to levels of individual, rather than population, risk. Because poor people tend to be less healthy their premiums, if

experience rated, will be higher in absolute terms and consequently *vis-à-vis* their income. Many will not be able to afford health care insurance. Low risk, and therefore low cost, customers will be drawn into low-premium plans, a process known as 'cream skimming'.

References

Brittan, L. (1988) *A New Deal for Health Care* (London: Conservative Political Centre).

Butler, E. and Pirie, M. (1988) *The Health of Nations* (London: Adam Smith Institute).

Culyer, A.J. (1991) 'The normative economics of health care finance and provision', in A. McGuire., P. Fenn and K. Mayhew, (eds) *Providing Health Care: The Economics of Alternative Systems of Finance and Delivery* 65–98. (Oxford: Oxford University Press).

Dearden, B. (1991) 'First welfare state at end of the road', *Health Service Journal*, 8 August, 15.

Donaldson, C. and Gerard, K. (1989) 'Countering moral hazard in public and private health care systems: a review of recent evidence', *Journal of Social Policy*, 18, 235–51.

Donaldson, C. and Gerard, K. (1993) *Economics of Health Care Financing: the Visible Hand* (London: Macmillan).

Evans, R.G. (1987) 'Public health insurance: the collective purchase of individual care', *Health Policy*, 7, 115–34.

Evans, R.G. (1990) 'Tension, compression and shear: directions, stresses and outcomes of health care cost control', *Journal of Health Politics Policy and Law*, 15, 101–28.

Farley, J.P. (1985) 'Who are the underinsured?', *Milbank Memorial Fund Quarterly*, 63, 476–503.

Farrar, S. (1993) 'NHS reforms and resource management: whither the hospital?', *Health Policy*, 26, 93–104.

Ginsburg, P.B. (1988) 'Public insurance programs: Medicare and Medicaid', in H.E. Frech III (ed.) *Health Care in America: the Political Economy of Hospitals and Health Insurance* (San Francisco: Pacific Research Institute for Public Policy).

Hakansson, S., Majnoni d'Intignano, B., Roberts, J. and Zollner, H. (1988) *The Leningrad experiment in health care management 1988.* Report of a visit to the USSR (Copenhagen: World Health Organisation).

Healey, A.T., Yule B. and Reid J.P. (1994) 'Variation in general practice prescribing costs and implications for budget setting', *Health Economics* 3, 47–56.

Himmelstein, D.U. and Woolhandler, S. (1986) 'Cost without benefit: administrative waste in the US health care system', *New England Journal of Medicine*, 314, 441–5.

Hopkins, A. (1992) 'Response to Mooney and Ryan', *Journal of Epidemiology and Community Health*, 46, 183.

Italian Ministry of Justice (1988) Legge 838: Institutzione del Sanitario, Supplement to Tazzotta Ufficcale, 28, December 1978, Rome 1978.

Letwin, O. and Redwood, J. (1988) *Britain's Biggest Enterprise* (London: Centre for Policy Studies).

Matsaganis M. and Glennerster H. (1994) 'The threat of "cream skimming" in the post-reform NHS', *Journal of Health Economics*, 13, 31–60.

Melnick, G.A. and Zwanziger, J. (1988) 'Hospital behaviour under competition and cost containment policies: the California experience, 1980 to 1985', *Journal of the American Medical Association*, 260, 2660–75.

Ministerio de Sanidad y Consumo (1989) *The Spanish Health System Highlights*, Direction General de Planeficacion Sanitoria, Madrid.

Mooney, G. and Salmond G. (1995) 'A reflection on New Zealand health care reform', *Health Policy*.

NHS Management Executive (1992) *Local Voices: the Views of Local People in Purchasing for Health* (London: NHS Management Executive.)

Palmer, G. and Short, S.D. (1989) *Health Care and Public Policy: an Australian Analysis* (Melbourne: Macmillan).

Quam, L. (1989) 'Post-war American health care: the many costs of market failure', *Oxford Review of Economic Policy*, 5, 113–23.

Richardson, J. (1987) 'Ownership and regulation in the health care sector', in P. Abelson (ed.), *Privatisation: an Australian Perspective* (Sydney: Australian Professional Publications).

Ryan, M. and Yule, B. (1993) 'The way to economic prescribing', *Health Policy* 25, 25–38.

Scott, C. (1994) 'Reform of the New Zealand health care system', *Health Policy* 29, 25–40.

Secretaries of State for Health Wales, Northern Ireland and Scotland, (1989) *Working for Patients* (London: HMSO).

Shackley, P. and Healey, A. (1993) 'Creating a market: an economic analysis of the purchaser–provider model', *Health Policy* 25, 153–68.

Sheldon, T. (1994) 'Public health reforms have failed, say Ministers', *British Medical Journal*, 308, 936.

Van de Ven W.M.M. (1989) 'A Future for Competitive Health Care in the Netherlands', NHS White Paper Series, Occasional Paper No. 9, Centre for Health Economics, University of York.

Wilensky, G.R. (1988) 'Filling the gaps in health insurance', *Health Affairs*, 7, 133–49.

Woolhandler, S. and Himmelstein, D.U. (1991) 'The deteriorating administrative efficiency of the US health care system', *New England Journal of Medicine*, 324, 1253–8.

3 Towards Effective Purchasing for Health: meeting the challenge

David J. Hunter

INTRODUCTION

After an uncertain start following the implementation of the NHS changes in 1991, purchasing is now viewed as the engine for change both in the future configuration of health care services and in the achievement of health gain for local populations. Purchasing's top place on the policy agenda was secured during 1993 when the then health minister, Dr Brian Mawhinney, sought to articulate in a series of keynote speeches the vision and direction for purchasing (Mawhinney and Nichol, 1993). For Mawhinney, 'purchasing is about change . . . Its importance lies in its capacity to anticipate and adapt to change' (ibid., pp. 3–4).

By the few accounts available of the purchasing role in practice, health authorities are some way from realising this goal. Indeed, many may never realise it. For many, purchasing has been about maintaining the status quo, resisting change and, at best, tinkering at the margins of current delivery systems and patterns of care (Klein, 1994). Acute services, which account for 51 per cent of all NHS spending, got 55 per cent of the funds available for new developments in the authorities surveyed by Redmayne, Klein and Day (1993) in 1992–3 and 58 per cent in 1993–4.

The 1994/5 purchasing plans are no different from their predecessors in 1992 and 1993 (Redmayne, 1995). A pattern of incremental, marginal change in the pattern of resource distribution looks set to continue. As Day and Klein argue in Redmayne (ibid., p. 7):

> . . . if the inherited pattern of spending priorities in the NHS is going to be modified, it will be the result not of dramatic shifts or convulsive changes but of a gradual, planned movement over time.

This outcome is not so surprising when you consider the novelty, enormity and complexity of the task. Moreover, it is rapidly becoming evident that the purchasing role as conceived lacks long term stability and looks set progressively to pass from district health authorities to GPs, principally fund-holders. Such a development, if it happens, would leave health authorities with a more strategic, outward looking commissioning role that is rather different from the purchasing, contracting role many currently have. The merger of DHAs and FHSAs to create new integrated authorities providing purchasing across the whole spectrum of health care will only hasten the shift to a more strategic focus. Joint commissioning arrangements with local authorities represent a further dynamic in the rapidly evolving nature of purchasing. Such arrangements tend to centre on community care provision but may also underpin health alliances established to secure *Health of the Nation* objectives.

Against this backcloth of political priority for purchasing combined with a redefinition of purchasing into operational (contracting) and strategic (commissioning) components, this chapter sets out to take stock of developments to date and to chart likely future developments. The focus throughout is on *effective* purchasing: what is it how can it be measured, and what are the barriers and constraints in respect of its achievement?

The rest of the chapter is in four sections. First, it is necessary to clarify terms and to establish what constitutes effective purchasing. For the purposes of this discussion, a distinction needs to be drawn between commissioning and purchasing. Often these terms are used interchangeably but, given the policy thrust towards a primary care-led NHS, a sharper distinction between the terms is necessary. Much of the content of the purchasing function will in future more appropriately fall within commissioning. **Commissioning** is the process of gathering and analysing the wants and needs of the population, and identifying the services required to meet those needs. **Purchasing** is the interpretation of commissioning plans, and the construction and implementation of time-related purchasing plans. Even with the gradual shift of purchasing to GPs, it is unlikely that health authorities will relinquish all their purchasing responsibilities. But the balance of these is intended to shift progressively towards commissioning from April 1996.

The next section reviews the experience of purchasing to date. There then follows an assessment of the key challenges confronting purchasers and the likelihood of these being successfully addressed. The chapter ends with a few speculative reflections on the potential for purchasing to survive in a climate where its mission seems almost certain to suffer from ambivalent political and public support, which ultimately could either severely compromise its potential to change the face of health care and health policy in the UK or neuter it altogether.

WHAT IS EFFECTIVE PURCHASING?

Put simply, the pre-1991 arrangements which conflated purchasing and providing functions in a single organisation were regarded as unsatisfactory for at least four reasons. First, they were prone to professional capture and operated as much for the benefit of those who worked in health services as for that of their clients. Second, they were potentially ineffective in contributing to health status since their focus was principally on health services, and acute ones at that, thereby ignoring for the most part the potential contribution of health promotion and public health measures. Third, integrated purchaser and provider bodies were unresponsive to client and public opinion more generally. Finally, there was only an indirect connection between revenue and workload with little incentive for efficiency.

The intellectual argument held that by separating the two functions matters would be improved in two ways:

- the new purchasing agency would be freed from provider vested interests as well as from day-to-day operational pressures which would allow it to be more proactive and innovative in the pursuit of effective health;
- the new agency could create competition between providers, thereby securing efficiency gains.

From the foregoing, a definition of effective purchasing goes something like this:

effective purchasing is the utilisation of the purchaser–provider split so as to embrace the effectiveness and cost-effectiveness of health care, responsiveness to the public and the efficiency with which resources are used. It is also likely to involve influencing agencies with a degree of control over variables which impact on health status. (Hunter and Harrison, 1993, p. 2)

As noted earlier, further complicating the purchasing function is the growing distinction between it and commissioning. In the early stages when the term commissioning crept into the vocabulary, it was often used interchangeably with purchasing but there is an important distinction to be made between them reinforced by developments in, and the expansion of, GP fund-holding. Hitherto, some health authorities have undertaken all the contracting and purchasing themselves while others (a growing number) have delegated substantial purchasing capacity and funding to GP practice groups. In between, various models and degrees of GP purchasing input, practice-sensitive and locality-based purchasing have emerged. In future, the expectation is that purchasing will be undertaken by GPs while health authorities will be responsible for commissioning and for giving support to GPs as well as monitoring their activities (NHS Executive, 1994 and 1995).

Mawhinney's seven 'stepping stones' to successful purchasing (see Box 1) combine both purchasing and commissioning responsibility but it is fair to say, on the basis of the evidence reviewed in the next section, that it is the second step – devising effective contracts – that has dominated purchasers' agendas with some attention to the first (given the requirement to produce five-year health strategies) and fifth – developing mature relations with providers – steps. The research and development strategy has for the most part still to make its mark on purchasing. There remains a lack of information about the effectiveness of services or procedures and their outcomes although this is the primary focus of the R and D strategy and the resources devoted to it. It may be that rationing would not be an issue if only effective procedures were offered, thereby releasing resources from ineffective interventions. The dilemma is in not knowing what is effective or ineffective. While the aspiration of knowledge based decision-making is commendable it will take time to achieve and will never be the final word on the subject. Medicine is an art as well as a science and professional judgement is unlikely to be replaced by hard-nosed evaluators. The R and D strategy, therefore, will not yield quick returns or prove conclusive.

Most purchasers are still struggling to consult their local communities and to find the most effective means of doing so. Again, progress is slow because accessing communities and developing a dialogue with

---

Box 1 Seven 'stepping stones' to purchasing

- Strategy

- Effective contracts

- Knowledge-base

- Responsiveness to local people

- Mature relations with providers

- Local alliances

- Organisational fitness

Source: Mawhinney and Nichol, 1993, p. 37.

---

them takes time and is far from simple or inexpensive (for a critical review of the issues see Gurney, 1994). Work in North Derbyshire over the past three years is a good example of the challenges and difficulties to be encountered (see Box 2).

Similar issues apply to the development of health alliances where, once again, the reality is one of limited progress.

Box 2 Involving local people: lessons from North Derbyshire Health Authority

- It is essential that consumerism is seen as an integral theme throughout the organisation. It should be the responsibility of *all* those involved in health purchasing and not only the research or health promotion functions.

- As the role of health purchaser continues to develop, a move away from an emphasis on illness should also develop. Issues around better health need a more systematic consumer input rather than just quality and quantity of local services.

- It is essential that local views are sought at an early enough stage for them to be used in developing strategies. Views obtained later in the process have a limited impact. Action must occur as a result of this work.

Contd.

Box 2 Contd.

- Health authorities cannot function in isolation but must work with others in the pursuit of health.

- Decisions on choosing priorities will have to be made and should reflect a full range of views and concerns.

- Consumers of health should be involved in 'outcomes' debates.

- Power must be shared with local people and groups. Health authorities do not always know best.

- Vulnerable groups of people should not be overlooked.

- Many people cannot speak for themselves and support for advocacy projects and initiatives should be given a high priority.

- Clear communications between the health authority and local people are essential.

- Support from the health authority to work with local people must continue. It must receive further priority if local people are to have a full role to play.

Source: North Derbyshire Health Authority, 1994.

EFFECTIVE PURCHASING: THE STORY SO FAR

As was mentioned in the Introduction, purchasing has some way to go to prove the theory that by separating purchaser from provider roles the liberating effect would be such that for the first time in the history of the NHS it would be possible to focus on effective health care and on non-curative, preventive measures. At the time of writing, the jury is still out on whether purchasing has a future and, if it does, its precise nature. The issue remains valid, only more so, in respect of the commissioning role being fashioned for the new health authorities after April 1996.

There has not been a great deal of empirical study of the 1991 NHS changes and it is of course too early to make any final pronouncements on their impact or outcome. Nevertheless, some four years into the changes it is legitimate to provide an interim assessment. Several small-scale studies and commentaries have appeared which set out to do precisely this (see, for example, Le Grand and Bartlett, 1993; Robinson and Le Grand, 1994; Tilley, 1993; Harrison and Freemantle,

1994). However, it remains the case that in debate over the NHS reforms 'anecdote and prejudice have generally substituted for systematic evaluation' (Le Grand, 1994, p. 260).

An economic survey of the UK carried out by the OECD (1994) includes a preliminary assessment of the NHS reforms. On purchasing, the survey comments that while districts are now able to think about local health needs and priorities, the split between purchasing and providing services 'is not yet always very sharp and the districts' purchasing function remains underdeveloped' (ibid., p. 75). One of the problems is that in districts with a single dominant provider it is difficult to maintain a clear separation between purchaser–provider roles. One study (Appleby *et al.*, 1994) of contracting in a region concluded that about a quarter of the hospitals in the region were in a pure monopoly situation. Another problem facing purchasers is a desire not to incur any political embarrassment which may flow from a decision not to contract on a large scale with a local hospital. Finally, many purchasers, far from driving the providers, are driven by them with providers telling them what is needed, in what volume and at what price.

Purchasers also suffer from other handicaps of a more far-reaching nature. While there is apparent widespread support for the health strategy, the *Health of the Nation*, which 'places the UK at the forefront of countries attempting to achieve more coherent health policies which recognise that health care is only one part – albeit an important one – in improving health' (OECD, 1994, p. 81), a major problem arises in seeking to reorient the NHS toward preventive measures especially when information on their effectiveness is weak.

There is also a problem over accountability, evident in the NHS Executive's Corporate Governance Task Force which produced codes in 1994 to reinforce public service values in health authorities and trust boards and to provide guidance on the conduct of their business. The government is sensitive to the charge that its NHS changes have created a democratic deficit by appointing party supporters to the authorities and boards responsible for the NHS and by unleashing a business ethic that is quite inappropriate in the NHS. But many within the NHS believe the problem goes deeper and strikes at the heart of the legitimacy of decision-making in the eyes of the public (Hunter, 1993). This applies particularly to the purchasers and it is argued that only by bringing them under local government control can the problem be solved (Harrison *et al.*, 1991; AMA, 1994; Clarke, Hunter and Wistow, 1994).

The problem of appropriate and robust information extends to other areas of purchasing, notably needs assessment. There is an absence of sound knowledge about the health needs of the population together with an inability to link this information to knowledge about where health care can make the greatest contribution to health status.

A study carried out for the NHSME in 1992 by the author and a colleague (Hunter and Harrison, 1993) required interviewing purchasers at all levels in two regions. A number of concerns were derived from the interviews. From the authors' knowledge and experience elsewhere they are neither uncommon nor unique to these regions. Among the more critical are those listed (in no particular order) in Box 3.

Box 3 Issues in purchasing

- the difficulty of articulating a strategic vision through lack of time, being diverted by demands of Region and centre, contradictions in government policy (e.g. efficiency index), the urgent forever driving out the important

- a lack of understanding of what outcome purchasing might mean and a tendency to equate it with *Health of the Nation* key targets

- a preoccupation with structure in the form of joint purchasing or commissioning arrangements, consortia, locality purchasing, DHA-FHSA mergers

- the finance-driven nature of the purchasing agenda

- the annual 'contracting treadmill' which absorbs senior management time for a couple of months or so

- over-dependence on single or a few providers; reluctance to challenge providers or clinical freedom

- public health uncertain of its role; performing unevenly but generally lacking grip on purchasing agenda

- health alliances slow to establish but demanding of senior management time

- the local government review is creating difficulties for collaborative working and is a source of 'planning blight'

Contd.

Box 3 Contd.

- concerns about the extent to which politicians at all levels are truly supportive of purchasers when they start to appreciate the possible implications for their electoral survival among the public who do not look kindly upon hospital cuts or closures, seeing them as attempts to dismantle their community infrastructure

- the loss of RHAs to the centre as outposts of the Department of Health makes DHAs more vulnerable because they represent the frontline and lack the protection the former RHAs could give them

- the R and D initiative is seen as critical to the success of purchasing and to giving it a sound knowledge base but it has been criticised for being too clinically biased and not being sufficiently HSR focused; there is a risk, too, of *research* overwhelming the importance of *development* and of managing behavioural change among clinicians

- links with the public remain weak and unfocused and ways of engaging with it are still in their infancy

- concern over explicit rationing exists when there is so much uncertainty over the effectiveness of medical interventions

- purchasing has not yet succeeded in shifting the health care paradigm from its traditional focus on services, and primarily those in the acute sector, to one in which health in its broader sense is uppermost.

Source: derived from Hunter and Harrison, 1993, pp. 2–3.

CHALLENGES AND CONSTRAINTS

To succeed and be effective, purchasing must develop in ways which break the mould with the past. If it fails to do so, questions will be asked about its value and politicians, ever anxious to reduce bureaucracy and allegedly unproductive layers of management, will rapidly switch their allegiance. Instead of looking upon purchasing as offering a way of advancing a genuine health policy as distinct from a health care one, they will condemn it for falling short of expectations and failing to deliver.

The intention to contain, and possibly reduce further, management costs is high on the Secretary of State for Health's priority list.

Purchaser development is necessary for the requisite skills and competencies to be acquired. Conventional management development based on practice in the private sector may be wholly inappropriate. For this reason, the notion of public health management has entered the vocabulary of purchasing (Alderslade and Hunter, 1992, pp. 21–2; Alderslade and Hunter, 1994). Public health management is concerned with mobilising society's resources, including the specific resources of the health service sector, to improve the health of populations. It is a loose and flexible notion, its true value lying in offering a common umbrella for the relevant groups and skills which can contribute to public health. As the Chief Medical Officer for England has argued, public health is 'an amalgamation of a series of 'ologies'' (Calman, 1993). He continues:

> There is no one single science and it must draw on molecular biology, clinical practice, sociology, education, politics, and management science. Hence the importance of team working and of using a wide range of skills to improve health.

Calman stresses the need for links between public health and non-medical disciplines, especially for putting the findings of public health medicine into practice. Developing the next generation of purchasers, or commissioners as they will probably become, is seen as a vital, yet neglected, area. In the study conducted by Hunter and Harrison (1993), a number of development issues and needs were expressed (see Box 4).

An Australian study investigating management competencies in the new public health settings found that certain qualities were seen as necessary in the effective public health manager (Lloyd, 1994). Charisma, commitment, and drive were identified as 'key figure' attributes as was the ability to function in a loosely regulated environment while simultaneously coping with bureaucratic processes. Coping with political issues was also seen as important if only because the new public health was political, in part because it had yet to become firmly established. The point is echoed in Eskin's (1991) view that to be effective public health physicians must be 'aware of the micro-political environment in which they work and actively use "people skills" or political skills in their daily work' (p. 65).

***Box* 4 Developing purchasing**

- the pressures on and the workloads of managers were too great and prevented the creation of time and forums to think strategically and longer term

- building and sustaining strong purchasing teams with the requisite skill mix was seen as essential

- separate career structures for purchasers and providers was not seen to be appropriate, secondments or attachments should be considered

- specific skills or competencies lay in negotiating, change management, health economics, communications, public health, management

- the development of the public health manager was a top priority.

Source: derived from Hunter and Harrison, 1993, pp. 9–10.

In monitoring purchaser performance, there is a strong case for adopting a more discursive approach in place of one which seeks to establish compliance with centrally determined hard targets (see Hunter and Harrison (1993) for an approach to monitoring purchasers). It is not a soft option since purchasers will be required to state what they have been trying to achieve, justify these claims, and assess their own success.

A number of internal organisational issues demand attention if the barriers to successful purchasing are to be confronted. The importance of public health medicine was noted earlier as well as some of the difficulties it has encountered. But, while its importance is widely acknowledged, there is also a degree of ambivalence and a strong sense of puzzlement on the part of many chief executives as to how the specialty should be used to best effect and integrated with the management perspective. It is a sense of puzzlement shared by many public health physicians (Richardson, Duggan and Hunter, 1994).

Consideration needs to be given to the development of forms of purchaser organisation which do not perpetuate traditional functional divisions; just because public health medicine is a specialty does not mean it has to be a department. Arguably, the Abrams report (Department of

Health, 1993) on the specialty makes it less likely that it will move to working in fluid and flexible organisational structures and yet this is what is needed to encourage the greater integration of all disciplines with a contribution to make to the purchasing function (Harris and Shapiro, 1994). Indeed, respondents in the study by Hunter and Harrison (1993) supported the development of project based structures in preference to departments or divisions. New arrangements for joint commissioning and the development of locality purchasing will increase the pressure for new ways of working and for employing a range of non-medical skills in the purchasing task.

The role of non-executive directors of purchasing authorities also needs developing in order to ensure that they are well-placed to assist in the analysis and determination of trade-offs between various aspects of effective purchasing. They should also be encouraged to participate in discursive monitoring of the kind mentioned above.

Finally, the R and D dimension should not be overlooked. It is of far greater importance than mere academic interest. Improving the knowledge base of decision-making was one of Mawhinney's seven 'stepping stones' for successful purchasing. The R and D effort requires focusing in order to maximise the impact of scarce research skills. Disseminating existing knowledge is essential, as exemplified by the successful series of Effective Health Care bulletins produced by Leeds and York Universities. There is a need, too, to target the research effort in directions likely to be of interest and relevance to purchasers. This means involving purchasers in the construction of research priorities in order to secure their ownership for it.

CONCLUDING OBSERVATIONS

The chapter opened with a reference to purchasing's somewhat uncertain origins and its even more uncertain future. The verdict on its value has yet to be delivered. It remains fragile and there can be no guarantee of its sustainability or longevity. A recent simulation – Rubber Windmill 4 – demonstrated that purchasing is 'weak, unable to develop skills fast enough, or reorientate [its] priorities to deal with the new world' (East Anglian RHA, 1994, p. 10). In the current state of policy turbulence, in which continuous change seems to be the only constant factor, it would be a rash observer who could predict with any confidence that purchasing will survive. It may, but it may not. Clearly, the chances of survival become greater if it can be demonstrated that it is working. Working in this context means delivering on the government's policy agenda and this is where the difficulties are at their most acute.

Government policy is rarely rational, coherent or unequivocal and any attempt at slavishly seeking to implement it risks falling foul of its internal contradictions, as well as the architects of that policy. Just as the policy to rationalise acute hospital services, close beds and hospitals in London has been modified, so it will be the case in other parts of the country where the attempt faithfully to implement pre-scribed policy clashes with the harsh realities of politics and the fickle-ness of an electorate who remain to be convinced of the benefits of closing hospitals and shifting much of what goes on in them to un-proven community-based primary care services. And in the absence of clear evidence that the shift is appropriate on the scale envisaged who can blame them for 'grabbing hold of nurse for fear of something worse'. Much current policy is aspirational in nature, and little more than an act of faith.

In this maelstrom of *realpolitik* and uncertainty it is hard to be opti-mistic about the future of purchasing or its strategic derivative, com-missioning. This observation applies regardless of which political party is in power since Labour has reaffirmed its commitment to retain-ing the purchaser–provider separation even if the details are unclear (Labour Party, 1995). The central point is that maybe the model itself is flawed. What works in at least parts of the commercial business sector may not be directly transferable to the public sector. It is interesting to observe how the talk in the NHS is increasingly, and akin to some of the practices evident in the private sector, of closer working between pur-chasers and providers. Indeed, in parts of the NHS the movement of managers between purchasers and providers, and vice versa, is being actively encouraged in order to ensure understanding of the two worlds. The emphasis is on long term collaborative relationships in which pre-ferred providers are identified (Redmayne, 1995). Whether this risks reintroducing the very cosiness and collusive behaviour which the separation of responsibilities was intended to end is a matter for further study. Perhaps it will not matter if the shift of power is in favour of purchasers rather than, as is the case presently, providers. Redmayne's (1995) review of health authorities' five year strategy documents leads her to conclude somewhat optimistically that it is not markets, competition or consumer preferences that are shaping the NHS of the next century but health authority planners using purchasing as their tool. Even if this optimistic assessment proves to be correct, the shift of purchasing to primary care could adversely affect progress in the desired direction.

Purchasing remains vulnerable on a broader level while we have yet to sort out as a society whether we wish to subject our public services to a hefty and undiluted dose of private sector managerialism or whether we wish to devise a model of organisation more appropriately derived from the experience of public sector services themselves. Regrettably, we are some way from articulating such a model. The task of doing so goes well beyond the scope of this chapter but until we succeed in finding such a model, purchasing will continue to remain vulnerable principally because it will operate in a context of such extreme political and managerial complexity and contradictions that the conflicting influences may in the end prove irreconcilable. The commissioning role of the new health authorities may offer the last chance for purchasing in its broad strategic sense to prove itself.

References

Alderslade, R. and D. Hunter (1992) 'Forward March', *Health Service Journal*, 102, 19 March, 22–3.

Alderslade, R. and D.J. Hunter (1994) 'Commissioning and Public Health', *Journal of Management in Medicine*, 8, No. 6, 20–31.

Appleby, J., P. Smith, W. Ranade, V. Little and R. Robinson (1994), 'Monitoring Managed Competition', in R. Robinson and J. Le Grand (eds), *Evaluating the NHS Reforms* (London: King's Fund Institute).

Association of Metropolitan Authorities (1994) *Local Authorities and Health Services: The Future Role of Local Authorities in the Provision of Health Services* (London: AMA).

Calman, K., *The Scientific Basis of Public Health* (1993) (Address to the Annual Conference of the Faculty of Public Health Medicine, Glasgow).

Clarke, M., D.J. Hunter and G. Wistow (1994) *Local Government and the National Health Service: The New Agenda* (London: Local Government Management Board).

Department of Health (1993) *Public Health: Responsibilities of the NHS and Roles of Others: Advice of the Committee Set up to Undertake a Review of HC(88)64)* (Abrams Report) (London: DoH).

East Anglian RHA (1994) *Power to the People?* Rubber Windmill 4 (Cambridge: East Anglian RHA).

Eskin, F. (1991) 'The Art of Public Health Medicine', *Public Health*, 105, 555–61.

Gurney, B.H. (1994) *Public Participation in Health Care*. A Report to the East Anglian RHA (Cambridge: Health Sciences Research Group, University of Cambridge).

Harris, A., and J. Shapiro (1994) 'Purchasers, Professionals, and Public Health', *British Medical Journal*, 308, 12 February, 426–7.

Harrison, S., D.J. Hunter, I.H. Johnston, N. Nicholson, C. Thunhurst and G. Wistow (1991) *Health Before Health Care*, Social Policy Paper No. 4 (London: Institute for Public Policy Research).

Harrison, S., and N. Freemantle (eds) (1994) *Working for Patients: Early Research Findings* (Leeds: Nuffield Institute for Health).

Hunter, D. (1993) 'No More Corporate Fudge', *Health Service Journal*, 103, 9 September, 20–2.

Hunter, D.J. and S. Harrison (1993) *Effective Purchasing for Health Care: Proposals for the First Five Years* (Leeds: Nuffield Institute for Health Services Studies).

Klein, R. (1994) 'Can we Restrict the Health Care Menu?', *Health Policy*, 27, 103–12.

Labour Party (1995) *Renewing the NHS* (London: The Labour Party).

Le Grand, J. (1994) 'Evaluating the NHS Reforms', in R. Robinson and J. Le Grand (eds), *Evaluating the NHS Reforms* (London: King's Fund Institute).

Le Grand, J. and W. Bartlett (1993) *Quasi-Markets and Social Policy* (London: Macmillan).

Lloyd, P. (1994) 'Management Competencies in Health for All/New Public Health Settings', *Journal of Health Administrative Education*, 12, 187–207.

Mawhinney, B. and D. Nichol, (1993) *Purchasing for Health: A Framework for Action* (Leeds: NHS Management Executive).

NHS Executive (1994) *Developing NHS Purchasing and GP Fundholding*, EL(94)79, (Leeds: NHS Executive).

NHS Executive (1995) *An Accountability Framework for GP Fundholding*, EL(95)54 (Leeds: NHS Executive).

North Derbyshire Health Authority (1994) *Listening and Responding to Local People* (Chesterfield: North Derbyshire Health Authority).

Organisation for Economic Cooperation and Development (OECD) (1994) *OECD Economic Surveys 1993–94: United Kingdom*, (Paris: OECD).

Redmayne, S. (1995) *Reshaping the NHS*, Research Paper No. 10 (Birmingham: National Association of Health Authorities and Trusts).

Redmayne, S., R. Klein and P. Day, (1993) *Sharing Out Resources* (Birmingham: National Association of Health Authorities and Trusts).

Richardson, A., M. Duggan and D.J. Hunter (1994) *Adapting to New Tasks: The Role of Public Health Physicians in Purchasing Health Care* (Leeds: Nuffield Institute for Health).

Robinson, R. and J. Le Grand (eds) (1994) *Evaluating the NHS Reforms* (London: King's Fund Institute).

Tilley, I. (ed.) (1993) *Managing the Internal Market* (London: Paul Chapman Publishing).

4 Purchasing in the NHS: administered or market contracts?

David Hughes, Lesley Griffiths and
Jean McHale

INTRODUCTION

Contract appears to be enjoying a renaissance in contemporary Britain. The legal theorist Patrick Atiyah (1995) has argued that the return to liberal market policies after 1979 was reflected in a revival of classical contract principles: that, as the wisdom of collective and bureaucratic decision making was challenged, the domain of activities covered by contract expanded at the expense of public regulation. Atiyah is concerned primarily with de-regulation and the resurgence of the doctrine of freedom of contract in private markets. However, if anything, 'contractualisation' has had an even more profound impact on the public services, which are undergoing the most radical re-structuring seen since the 1940s. The increasing scope of the contract principle is apparent both in the growth of 'contracting out' since the early 1980s, and experiments with internal markets and other quasi-market variants in the 1990s (Harden, 1992; Le Grand and Bartlett, 1993; Harrison, 1993; Vincent-Jones, 1994a; 1994b; Hudson, 1994; Tam, 1994). 'Market testing', 'franchising' and 'management contracts' are other specific mechanisms that have developed out of competitive tendering.

The widespread use of the language of 'contract' in the public sector does not necessarily mean that the governance of exchange relationships is contractual in the conventional legal sense. It is used to cover many different organisational arrangements, including rather traditional relationships of hierarchical accountability. The new public-sector contracts do not always arise from the voluntary choices of the parties, they may leave the parties only limited freedom to determine terms, and they are often not enforceable as legal contracts. Harrison

(1993) suggests that these contracts represent a reformulation of market relations within a public-sector hierarchy. They retain some of the incentive properties and formality of conventional contracts, without implying a full switch to market relations and contract law.

Although many aspects of 'private law' contracting are absent in these public-sector transactions, there are several reasons why it could be premature to assert their non-contractual nature. One is that the parties themselves may emphasise the reality of the 'contract', and model their behaviour according to their perceptions of contracting in other sectors. Another is that public quasi-markets often incorporate mechanisms, such as 'arbitration' procedures, that resemble the arrangements found in private markets. A third is that many quasi-markets are subject to significant penetration by private providers, so that 'real' contracts between public and private enterprises exist alongside contracts within public institutions, with the possibility that common approaches may develop.

This paper introduces empirical evidence from the National Health Service (NHS) to examine the nature of contracting in what many consider to be the prototypical internal market system. We explore parallels with academic models of contracting, specifically, with the classical, neo-classical, relational and administered contract models. NHS contracts are heavily regulated, but parties nevertheless recognise certain parallels with market contracting. They have developed working constructs which, whether intentionally or not, draw differentially on these different approaches. Practice appears to be remarkably diverse, with some purchasers and providers placing more emphasis than others on the centrality of written contracts and the need for precise drafting. We pay special attention to a Welsh District Health Authority (DHA) – 'Alpha' – which is well-known for its robust line on contracts and is said to have gone as far as any in Wales towards implementing a 'business-like' approach.

Our data are drawn from a three-year study of NHS contracting in Wales that is still ongoing. The findings reported here come mainly from the first phase of the research, which involves observations of Alpha's core contract team meetings, and its contract negotiation and monitoring meetings with providers. Some additional information comes from semi-structured interviews with the nine Welsh DHAs and the 22 Welsh NHS Trusts listed in the 1994/5 Health Services Year Book, which constitute the second phase of the study.

THE NHS REFORMS

The *National Health and Community Care Act, 1990* (see Longley 1990; Hughes 1991; Jacob 1991) modified the traditional tiered structure of the NHS by establishing a split between purchasers and providers of health care. DHAs were required to reduce their involvement in provision and concentrate on a service commissioning role. General practice fund-holders (GPFHs) also have a purchasing role. Hospitals and other units were encouraged to apply for NHS Trust (NHST) status and move outside DHA control, attracting funds through service contracts. The result, in theory at least, is an internal market in which DHAs and GPFHs purchase health care from a range of competing providers, including NHSTs, the remaining directly-managed units (DMUs) and the private sector. In the period since the implementation of the Act a number of DHAs have come together in purchasing commissions, and recent legislation allowed DHAs and FHSAs to formally merge from April 1996. In practice, many DHAs, including Alpha, were already purchasing in partnership with FHSAs.

At face value the reforms represented an attempt to apply the 'contract culture' to the heart of the welfare state. Contracts are the mechanism chosen by government to structure relationships between the different entities making up the NHS. The framework set out in early guidance (DH, 1989a; 1989b; 1990) envisaged that contracts would fall into three main categories. The first, contracts between NHS purchasers and private sector providers, take a conventional legal form and have been commonplace in the NHS for some years, especially where services were purchased using waiting-list initiatives' money. The second, service agreements between DHAs and their DMUs, structured as contracts but enforced through normal management processes, have virtually disappeared with the move to NHST status. By 1994/5, the third category – NHS contracts – covered the bulk of purchased activity. These are agreements for the provision of clinical services between NHS bodies who have no direct management relationship, such as contracts between DHAs and NHSTs, and all GPFH contracts. NHS contracts have attracted a good deal of scholarly commentary (Hughes, 1990; Longley, 1990; Appleby, 1994; Harden and Longley, 1995; Allen, 1995). It has been noted, *inter alia*, that the parties are public entities, not independent actors; the terms of the contracts are largely determined by statute and regulation; the parties often negotiate from a position of bilateral monopoly; disputes in pre-contract negotiations can be submitted to special arbitration procedures; and the contracts are not judicially enforceable. To date, empirical data on NHS contracts in action – what goes on inside the 'black box' of the contracting process – is limited to a few exploratory studies (Cohen, 1994; Ferlie, 1994; Laughlin *et al.*, 1994; Flynn, Pickard and Williams, 1995). This chapter is intended as a further contribution to the emerging body of evidence.

MODELS OF CONTRACTING

Before considering our empirical data, it will be necessary to review some of the academic models of contracting behaviour. An influential three-way classification devised by the lawyer Ian Macneil (1978), and taken up by the economist Oliver Williamson (1979; 1981), distinguishes between classical, neo-classical and relational categories of contract law. These may be seen as ideal types that can be applied to contracting behaviour in private markets, but given their influence in contract scholarship, there is an obvious possibility that their influence has spread to the analysis of contracting in quasi-market environments like the NHS. Additionally in the light of the distinctive forms of planning and regulation that affect the NHS, we also include a fourth model: the administered contract.

(i) Classical contract law

The emergence of classical contract law coincided with the rise of free market economics. As Lawrence Friedman (1965, 20–4) has observed: 'In both theoretical models ... parties could be treated as individual economic units which in theory enjoyed complete mobility and freedom of decision'. Contracts were a legal instrument for managing the uncertainty of market relationships by limiting risks to those calculated by the parties. The terms of a contract were to be formal and external, conveying a determinant meaning independent of the subjective intentions of the parties. To enter into a contract was to make a legally binding promise, which could be enforced in the courts, normally with the sanction of compensatory monetary damages.

Macneil (1978, 862–5) argues that classical contract law supports economic exchange by enhancing the 'discreteness' of the transaction and intensifying 'presentation' – the specification in the present contract of events or contingencies that may affect future contract performance. A discrete transaction may be defined as one in which no duties exist between the parties until these duties are specified in a contract. The discrete transaction is an attractive analytical unit for economists because it allows manageable calculations of risk and benefit. Complications such as the identities of the parties and matters external to the contract can be largely ignored. Presentation similarly facilitates rational calculations of risk. It implies that the contract accurately specifies what will happen if the agreement is breached, or if contingencies arise that prevent the parties from performing their duties. The classical model therefore directs our attention to a series of single transactions shaped by short-term, utility-maximising behaviour, which are underpinned by formal contract documents, legal rules and remedies provided in the courts.

Few would dispute the heuristic power of the classical model and the theoretical advances it has brought in law and economics. Nevertheless there is a growing acknowledgement that many contractual relationships, particularly those which have long duration and involve transaction-specific investments, may be more fruitfully analysed using different frameworks.

(ii) Neo-classical contracts

There are many situations where future contingencies cannot be anticipated, where the drafting of 'complete' contracts would be prohibitively costly or impossible, and where monitoring is difficult because the same information is not available to both parties. One way of dealing with these problems is to move to a different contract form with a modified 'neo-classical' governance structure. Macneil (1978, 865) describes how many long-term contracts rely on 'a range of processes and techniques used by contract planners to create flexibility in lieu of either leaving gaps or trying to plan rigidly'. These techniques function to increase the confidence of the parties in settlement processes and keep contracts alive even under conditions of uncertainty. Examples include use of external standards validated and updated by third-parties, third-party determination of performance through arbitration rather than litigation, agreements to let one party set or update particular terms (for example, right of termination), agreements that price will be based on provider costs, and 'agreement to agree' clauses. Such techniques help parties to manage the indefiniteness of contracts by identifying external benchmarks for performance, specifying agreed settlement processes that are not disruptive of the trading relationship, or enhancing confidence by guaranteeing the freedom of one or other of the parties to fill gaps in agreed areas. Neo-classical contracts retain the basic structure of classical contracts, but represent a relaxation of rigorous presentiation and an attempt to encourage the continuation of a relationship in the face of trouble. For example, dispute settlement clauses in neo-classical contracts typically not only specify an arbitration procedure, but provide that performance of the contract continues pending the outcome of arbitration.

(iii) Relational contracts

Pressures to maintain long-term business relationships in the modern economy mean that use of neo-classical contract drafting strategies has become common, but many theorists argue that the parties' concern with the ongoing relationship is often so central that a different 'relational' contract model emerges. While classical or neo-classical contracts are about an explicit allocation of risks between the parties, relational contracts are about planning an ongoing relationship. The emphasis is less on the contract as a legal document underpinned by formal enforcement in the courts, than as a reference point for administrative processes of monitoring and adjustment which structure the relationship. Discreteness and presentiation are not entirely displaced as concerns, but they become two norms among many others regulating the relationship. In Macneil's (1978, 901) terms, the relationship becomes 'a mini-society with a vast array of norms beyond the norms centring on exchange and its immediate processes'. In contrast to the neo-classical contract, where the reference point for changed arrangements is the original contract, the reference point in a relational contract system is the entire relationship as it has developed over time.

Long-term contracts of this kind incorporate an open-ended approach which facilitates subsequent variation or renegotiation of obligations. A wide range of specific drafting techniques may be used to achieve this end, all ultimately turning on a commitment to co-operation in pursuing joint goals (Macneil, 1975; Campbell and Harris, 1993). While this approach implies the loss of the legal remedies provided by classical contract law, contracts can become more flexible and easily revised – 'clarity being rejected in favour of productive ambiguity' (Campbell and Harris, 1993, p. 169).

(iv) Administered contracts

As Freidmann (1975) and others have pointed out, certain ideal type characteristics of the classical contract model have been eroded by the development of institutional relations in the modern economy. The terms on which contracts are made and enforced have become matters for economic and social policy and a degree of governmental intervention. In consequence the limits of liability, whether inside or outside the contract, are affected by many considerations beyond the terms of the agreement. If anything the nature and scope of contract regulation in Britain has increased in recent years, particularly in relation to contracts between the public and private sectors and the regulated market regimes created for many of the privatised enterprises. While those who support a classical approach have tended to view regulation as antithetical to the contracting paradigms outlined above (see, for example, Posner, 1969), there are others who take a more revisionist stance, seeing regulation as a necessary evil which can be tolerated as long as its distorting effects on market processes are controlled (Vickers and Yarrow, 1989). At the extreme, though, there is the possibility that regulation may erode certain of the defining features of contract to the point where the continued use of the term becomes theoretically controversial.[1]

An apposite example, which excited much interest in Western contract scholarship in the 1960s and 1970s, is contracting between economic enterprises in the Soviet Union. Transactions between these enterprises were expected to accord with a central planning document (the nariad) issued by a procurement and marketing agency, but the details of the arrangement were set out in a contract signed by the parties, and enforced through a special regime of state arbitration boards. While the parties retained a degree of freedom in negotiating precise terms, matters such as price and quality were determined by state-established tariffs and standards, and the negotiation of a contract with the nominated partner was compulsory (Hazard, 1969, p. 354).[2] The significant point for our purposes concerns the controversy that arose regarding the status of these contracts. From one perspective, such agreements were merely 'sham contracts', since they were 'controlled by the general plan and various directives from top agencies [and did] not express the free will and individual initiative of the executives' (Gsovski, 1948, quoted by Speer, 1971). However, for other commentators, the contract represented a decentralised mechanism for matching plan with local circumstances (Berman, 1963), a mechanism for creating civil law obligations for the parties (Loeber, 1964), and an indication of how 'efficiency considerations influence the choice of contract rules even in a system where the market has been displaced by central planning' (Kroll, 1987, p. 124). There is argument, even among Soviet legal scholars, regarding whether the state arbitration boards which regulate these contracts are to be seen as judicial or administrative bodies imposing legal or managerial controls (Pomorski, 1977). Contracts between Soviet economic enterprises may thus be seen as an extreme comparator to the market contracts examined earlier, located at the far fringes of contract scholarship, yet possessing intriguing parallels with recent Western attempts to use market-type structures in public sector environments, whose status may generate similar controversy.[3]

In Britain, innovations of this kind can be traced back to attempts to improve management in government by the reform of the central departments. The framework agreements used by Next Steps Agencies were one early attempt to develop contract-like arrangements. Service level agreements in local government, and the agreements between the operating sectors of British Rail in the immediate pre-privatisation period are other examples. The creation of a special class of NHS contracts, defined in statute and underpinned by a statutory dispute resolution procedure, may be seen as an extension of this trend.

FINDINGS FROM ALPHA DISTRICT

How do these contracting models equate with practice as observed in our case study? While Department of Health (DH) guidance (DH 1989b; 1990) established a clear procedural framework for contracting, it was much less explicit about the form contracting relationships should take. As the market developed, it became clear that individual purchasers and providers were pursuing widely divergent approaches (Raftery and Gibson, 1994). Some equated good contracting with arm's length relationships, competition and robust bargaining, and stressed the binding nature of contracts and the need for strict monitoring and enforcement. Others rejected this 'adversarial' approach and instead highlighted the need for purchasers and providers to work co-operatively as 'partners' within a common management process. Our early research in Wales suggests that there is indeed a range of practice. According to informants in the Welsh Office (WO) and other DHAs, Alpha is the most adversarial of the Welsh districts in its approach to contracting. The DHA prides itself on its long record of progressive management and has moved to implement the reform programme with more enthusiasm than many other authorities. Some friction has arisen with providers over Alpha's tough approach to contract monitoring, and particularly its insistence on the insertion of penalty clauses in contracts. The approach taken, certainly at the time our research started, contrasted noticeably with that of other DHAs who felt sanctions within contracts were unnecessary and, in a few cases, sought to foster the long-term nature of relationships by implementing preferred provider arrangements and three-year rolling contracts. Alpha therefore exemplifies a DHA which has opted for a version of contracting that tries to borrow certain features – like penalties – from business contracts.

Relations with providers have fluctuated but have never been 'cosy'. Respondents reported that after a difficult period in the first two years of the internal market relations began to improve, and this was reflected in the scheduling of meetings with main providers at monthly rather than quarterly intervals. However, in 1994/5 there was a particularly acrimonious dispute with a local provider that changed things for the worse. Several monitoring meetings were cancelled and they again became less frequent. There were conflicts over Alpha's alleged attempts to monitor unit activity in a way that bypassed unit management, over quality of information, and claims that units were manipulating activity returns to hide under-performance. More recently, following some changes of personnel, bridges are again being re-built.

Notwithstanding Alpha's tough approach to contracting, it would be wrong to characterise its position as one of naked utility maximisation or 'macho management'. Senior officers see arm's length relationships and robust bargaining as the best route to follow if the NHS reforms are to be made to work. They take the view that this is the most effective of the limited number of options available to them, but emphasise that the approach is moderated by reasonableness. Penalties have been balanced by informal rewards ('motivation investments') in terms of developments and waiting list monies, and have not been levied when reasonable explanations for infractions were forthcoming. It is worth emphasising that as far as our own dealings with DHAs in Wales as researchers is concerned, Alpha has proved to be more co-operative, open and consistent than some other DHAs which claimed to be at the softer end of the contract spectrum.

Although Alpha has a contracts manager, the contracting team is led by the Director of Finance. The authority never used the simple block contracts reported elsewhere (Ferlie, 1992; Cohen, 1994) and portrays its favoured contract form as a variety of cost and volume contract. The same basic contract format is used for all the major providers, including both NHSTs and DMUs. In outline, these contracts take the form of a single annual agreement which specifies volumes of activity for each specialty, under the three headings of in-patients, day cases and new out-patients. Contract payments are made by monthly instalments and activity per specialty is constantly monitored. Departures of more than two per cent above or below agreed levels trigger action. If agreed volumes are exceeded the authority must decide whether to authorise extra payments at agreed marginal rates, or to instruct the unit to curtail activity. Where there is a shortfall in activity, payments are normally reduced on a full cost rather than marginal cost basis. Alpha has only two block contracts: one with a hospital in an adjoining district for cystic fibrosis work and one for community services, both of which were considered to present special problems resistant to the use of cost and volume approaches. Alpha uses a different contract form for private providers, which was originally adapted from its procurement contracts with professional legal assistance, and contains indemnity clauses.

(i) Classical elements

If presentation and discreteness are the key elements of the classical approach, how discernable are they in Alpha's practice? The 1994/5 standard contract is a 12-page document with an appended 21-page quality schedule. Detailed contract provision is not necessarily the same as presentation, but many of the clauses appear to have been written to ensure that contract performance is kept within predictable limits. Private sector contracts frequently incorporate a range of techniques at the planning stage that aim to facilitate monitoring and enforcement of performance, including instalment payments, inspection, forfeitures, deposits, and agreed damages. Alpha's contracts specify monthly payment dates, and make provision for 'quality visits' to provider sites. Special attention is given to contingencies that may affect price: the inflation uplift is restricted to an agreed figure, the provider must give three months notice of materials price rises, and it is stated that 'there shall be no variation in prices during the year other than that provided for in the terms of the contract'. The provider is required to price services on the basis of full costs for all purchasers, with the exception of short-term spare capacity, which must be offered in the first instance to Alpha and local GPFHs. Activity purchased in each specialty is specified in a schedule and there are clauses setting out the procedures to be followed if and when variations occur. Where 'under-performance' occurs, the amount deducted from the contract sum differs according to circumstance: it is based on full costs of treatments where patients remain on waiting lists, on an agreed variable cost calculation for most other speciality work, and on a marginal cost calculation where new service developments are involved. Other clauses address the problem of opportunistic behaviour. For example, the provider is required to keep a record of all patients medically cleared for discharge not discharged within 48 hours, and it is stated that any consequent contract variation is subject to specific agreement.

Despite its quest for relatively complete contracts, Alpha makes frequent use of contract variations as a preferred alternative to new contracts. Far from being an occasional solution to inadequate contract planning, this is an accepted part of contracting strategy. The authority retains a reserve to buy additional activity on a flexible basis as the need arises through the year, and will also be alert to the possibility of using waiting list monies to buy activity at agreed marginal costs through contract variations, rather than new contracts.

Alpha's attitude to presentation is therefore somewhat ambiguous. It continues to emphasise the need for precise and rigorous drafting, but uses a contract form that is readily adaptable and is indeed designed to be so. After initially favouring contracts containing very detailed clauses, Alpha explored ways of simplifying and shortening contract documentation. The expansion of the quality schedule to include Patient's Charter and other targets had been seen as a particular problem, and a separate 'quality directory' was produced, defining standards that all potential contractors were required to meet, and allowing the contract to be slimmed down.

If there is evidence of a concern with presentation, what of discreteness? An important feature of the discrete transaction model is that many potential trading partners exist, and the parties to a contract give no guarantees that it will be renewed. That is to say that discreteness is linked to competition. In Alpha, as in many districts, competition could occur only in respect of a limited volume of elective work that might be performed by providers outside the local area, by private hospitals, or, in a few areas, by more than one of the main providers. Alpha has used external providers only rarely, usually in respect of specialist services not available locally, or where waiting list initiative monies were allocated to remove backlogs in local hospitals. There has been little serious debate about moving core business away from the main providers. The rolling forward of contracts from one year to the next has more of the character of old-style uplifting of the short-term plan than of a bidding process in which external providers participate. Respondents suggested that one-off contracts using waiting list monies with distant providers were occasionally used as a lever to get local consultants to improve performance. However, in 1994/5, only one longer-term contract[4] (for rheumatology out-patient services), which might have been met locally, was placed with an external provider. Overall Alpha officers were unenthusiastic about use of distant hospitals, pointing to patients' unwillingness to travel, problems of monitoring contracts, and their continuing sense of obligation to local providers.

(ii) Neo-classical elements

The neo-classical model represents a development of, rather than a radical departure from the classical model, and provides for the long-term nature of contracts by providing 'internal' contract mechanisms to prevent relationship breakdown. Parties can, for example, refer to external standards that will be periodically updated, or specify the use of adjustment mechanisms or alternative dispute settlement arrangements, short of the courts. Alpha's contracts include no requirement for third-party accreditation such as the King's Fund scheme, or reference to external performance standards, but two prominent neo-classical elements are present in the shape of financial penalties and an arbitration clause.

Penalty clauses represent a kind of 'internal law' operated by the parties themselves. The courts in Britain and the United States have generally been unwilling to enforce penalties. But, like classical techniques, penalties may be seen as a sanction within the contract (and the discrete transaction) rather than a sanction imposed by changing the terms of the long-term relationship. Alpha's ability to make penalty clauses stick is therefore a revealing test of the viability of the discrete transaction approach.

Modest penalties for under-performance were introduced in 1992/3, but their scope and size has since been increased. By 1994/5 the penalty for failure to meet *Patient's Charter*[5] wait times had risen to £10000 per infraction, while failure to notify the purchaser of excessive waits incurred a penalty of £5000.[6] Smaller monetary penalties are also imposed for failure to provide monitoring information within agreed timescales or returning incomplete or inaccurate information.

Alpha had deducted more than a quarter of a million pounds in penalties by the start of 1994/5, and senior officers remain convinced of their effectiveness in improving performance. However, the strategy provoked considerable friction with providers. At one stage in 1993–4 the Director of NHS Wales wrote formally to notify the Chief Executive of the concern expressed by providers, but stopped short of intervening. What proved more difficult to resist was pressure from providers who were able to use market position to extract concessions. Two providers of specialist services in Wales threatened to handle Alpha patients on an extra contractual referral only basis (at significantly higher unit prices) unless penalties were dropped. Following an approach by one of these providers, WO sent a second letter requiring that a contract be agreed. Alpha reluctantly agreed to reduce contract penalties to nominal levels for this provider, and shortly afterwards similar arrangements were made with the second external provider. Currently, none of Alpha's main local providers have forced similar concessions. Any chance they had of doing so in 1995/6 was effectively undermined when other nearby purchasers adopted similar penalties.

NHS contract disputes are subject to a statutory arbitration procedure, and Alpha's contracts contain an arbitration clause. NHS guidance[7] indicates that parties should name an agreed arbitrator to whom disputes can be referred in the first instance, but in fact Alpha's contracts merely state that either party 'shall be entitled to take recourse to the agreed NHS processes of arbitration should there be a failure to agree on any major aspect of this contract'. Despite its reputation for adversarial relations, Alpha has not been involved in arbitration and only gone to conciliation on one occasion. Notwithstanding this, Alpha is perceived by WO as an authority that has its fair share of contract wrangles, and the non-use of arbitration may be attributed to strong WO pressure to settle problems informally. We discuss dispute settlement in more detail below.

(iii) Relational elements

Campbell and Harris (1993) have commented that long-term contracts display three characteristics. First, legal documents tend to be open ended and display rejection of presentation in favour of explicit flexibility. Second, there is recourse to extra-legal strategies to handle problems which cannot be dealt with under the legal documents. Third, parties will in all but the most extreme cases adopt co-operative strategies.

As we have seen, Alpha has attempted to draft relatively complete contracts and, although concerns have been raised about over-complexity, senior officers regard claims about the advantages of open-endedness with scepticism. However, there is a good deal of evidence of a more relational approach with respect to the remaining two characteristics. While Alpha's contract documents take a broadly classical form, this is less true of the behaviour that surrounds the contract.

Recourse to extra-legal strategies to handle problems not dealt with in the contract is made in a number of contexts. It is clear that, for Alpha and its main providers, contracts are embedded in long term relationships which include understandings that lie outside any single contract and often relate to local health care plans and strategies that pre-date the contract round. Alpha's main providers have expectations about the overall pattern of services in the area and support for particular specialities on particular sites, that surface from time to time in contract negotiation meetings and help shape contracts. It is also evident that the 'deal' agreed with an individual unit for the year often includes understandings that are not written down in the contract. Alpha officers talk of 'motivation investments' (additional payments) that can be used to reward good contractual performance, and which may be perceived by providers as part of the overall settlement. In one observed case, a favourable price appears to have been balanced against an (extra-contractual) undertaking to transfer more activity to that provider in future years. At a more mundane level, there were examples of 'gentlemen's agreements' to trade off under-performance in some specialties against over-performance in others as the year progressed.

Willingness to adopt co-operative strategies is affected by the identity of the contracting partner. In 1994/5 Alpha was still protective of its remaining DMUs, which were being prepared for trust status in the following year. It tended to adopt a less aggressive tone in bargaining, and to use contracts strategically to manage the problems of individual units. For example, Unit 'C' faced financial and organisational difficulties following the rejection of a major expansion plan and the relocation of some acute activity to other sites. Steps were taken to facilitate its amalgamation with Unit 'D' by ensuring a viable contract portfolio, including contracts for community services. Trust 'B' which had recently attained NHST status was regarded jealously by 'A' (an established trust), which claimed that Alpha had supported 'B' in specialties where the two competed, despite higher prices. Providers in turn appeared more willing to concede ground in dealings with their main commissioners than with peripheral purchasers. An area where this issue came up was in connection with over-performance on contracts. Unit 'C' acceded to Alpha's request to complete additional work at marginal rates, but refused to do the same for neighbouring Beta district.

One general set of pressures pushing the parties towards co-operation is the poor quality of the monitoring information available from most units. Alpha was perceived by providers as one of the most demanding Welsh districts in this respect, but it nevertheless had to make compromises. In many instances obviously deficient activity data were allowed to stand as a proxy for the more systematic information originally demanded. Sometimes Alpha officers were forced to accept a straightforward appeal to trust as the only way of making progress.

The growing power of GPFHs as purchasers has created an additional incentive for the development of co-operative strategies. Fundholders are in an important sense the 'wild cards' in the internal market. They more than other players have the opportunity to shop around and to approach individual contracts as single transactions. The transfer of monies from DHAs to GPFHs introduces a degree of unpredictability into local purchasing patterns and constitutes a potential risk to the

Health Plans that Welsh DHAs are required to produce. There is uncertainty about what monies GPFHs have available, how they are spending it, and the flow of money through the financial year. In self-defence DHAs and providers co-operate to share information on GP purchasing and to deal with problems that are thrown up. One problem centres on fund-holder underspending of revenue earmarked for certain treatments, such as hip and knee surgery, with the result that hospitals are performing below expected activity levels even though DHA funds are exhausted. Prior to the 1994/5 contract round, WO had reclaimed some unspent money from GPFHs for re-distribution to DHAs. With the expectation that this pattern would be repeated, Alpha reached (unwritten) understandings with some providers that those willing to 'over-perform' on contracts would get any re-distributed funds.

(iv) Administered elements

This category brings us to Alpha's relationship with WO, and the nature of the wider contracting environment. Purchasers and providers enter NHS Contracts because they are required by statute to do so, but many aspects of contracting are subject to ongoing regulation from the centre. It is widely acknowledged that the 1991 reforms strengthened the chain of command from Secretary of State to the DHAs. Moreover NHSTs, despite their devolved freedoms, are required to comply with directions and circulars from the central departments (1990 Act, Schedule 2, para. 6(2)). There has been a steady stream of directives on matters such as cost allocation principles for pricing (Dawson, 1994), arrangements for intervention in the case of late payments, an instruction that the 'market testing' of appropriate services should be specified in contracts, and a requirement to incorporate *Patient's Charter* standards in contracts.

WO has adapted most of the English guidance on contracting, but has favoured a rather different strategic approach. The NHS Directorate has assumed a key role in 'managing the market' (WO, 1992, Chapter 3). Commissioners stand in a line management relationship with the Directorate, and are required to agree a strategic framework for the delivery of health gain and develop local strategies for health and health plans. NHSTs are accountable to the Secretary of State, through the Director of NHS Wales, and must prepare rolling five year plans linked to local health strategies. The flavour of these arrangements is well captured in a 1992 letter from a senior official to DGMs on the topic of openness in contracting:

> We see NHS Wales as a 'managed trading organisation', with individual trusts and DMUs as constituent parts of this single corporation. Openness cannot therefore be left as a matter for local discretion.

Contracting has been placed within the established framework of planning for 'health gain', and much of the Strategic Management Division's work in the contract field has been concerned with refining service specifications in areas linked to health gain targets. Model service specifications have been developed in five specialties, together with related outcome indicators.

The various rules affecting HAs and NHSTs are differentially enforced according to a hierarchy of perceived importance. At the time of the research, in Wales as in England, Patient's Charter guarantees on patient waiting times were given very high priority. In Wales these were supplemented by additional local waiting time standards, based on WO's *Caring for the Future* document. The introduction of more demanding Charter guarantees in 1994/5 is regarded by some of our respondents as a pivotal development that fundamentally changed the balance of power between purchasers and providers. Purchasers using cost and volume, or sophisticated block, contracts typically shifted risks arising from increasing volumes of activity to providers by specifying that additional payments would be at the purchaser's discretion. However, the fact that purchasers now became directly accountable to WO for the success of a high-profile political initiative on waiting times, put them under great pressure to ensure that providers had the resources to meet unfunded increases in activity that would otherwise feed through into waiting lists. WO in turn committed substantial waiting list initiative funds to help deal with this problem. Taken together, these developments illustrate how, within the NHS internal market, bilateral 'contractual' relations intersect with hierarchical administrative relationships, which are largely invisible within individual NHS contracts but significantly affect relations between the contracting parties.

The administrative centre has also taken steps to influence the currency used in NHS contracts. WO, like the DH, has been concerned that

most health authorities have been slow in moving beyond contracting on the basis of uplift of historic budgets ('roll-over') towards an
approach that genuinely reflects provider tariffs and the costs of services. While the DH has opted for Health Resource Groups (HRGs)
as the route to case-mix sensitive purchasing, WO favours a version of
Diagnosis Related Groups (DRGs). However WO's original requirement that HAs use DRGs as a contract currency from April 1995
ran into difficulties because of information deficits and service
opposition on both sides of the purchaser–provider split. At the time
of writing, WO requires a move to a generic currency of provider
spells in April 1996, with DRG information available in shadow
form.

Within this general strategic framework, WO has been prepared to
allow a measure of local diversity. Alpha's more adversarial approach
has been tolerated, despite complaints from some providers. The WO
Health Department has been reluctant to intervene directly except
where the integrity of the internal market was seen to be threatened.
During the study period Alpha was instructed to contract for a specialist
service already available to GPFH patients in its area, so as to avoid the
emergence of a 'two-tier service'. Other communications in respect of
penalty clauses were mentioned above, and there was also contact in
respect of Alpha's tough line on ECR payments. Elsewhere, WO took
action to stop DHAs putting pressure on units to shut out GPFHs. Officers in Alpha and elsewhere are thus left in little doubt that institutional
constraints on contracting apply. Overall though, the extent of intervention is not so great that purchasers and providers lose all sense of
a bilateral contracting relationship. In fact, five of the 22 NHSTs
surveyed said there were no occasions when they had contacted, or
been contacted by, WO following problems in contract negotiations or
subsequent disputes.

DISPUTE SETTLEMENT

Markets and bureaucratic hierarchies handle disputes in different ways.
Disputes between enterprises in private markets are typically settled
through informal negotiations between the parties themselves or, at the
extreme, through arbitration or litigation. Disputes within administrative hierarchies may again be resolved informally, but are also com-

monly dealt with through bureaucratic regulation – the top-down enforcement of rules via administrative processes and internal disciplinary procedures. At face value, the dispute resolution arrangements for NHS contracts combine elements of both approaches. There are limited parallels with commercial arbitration but also much potential for the exercise of power by the central departments. Much depends on how the arrangements set out in statutory instrument and guidance are applied. Dispute settlement thus provides a particularly revealing 'window' for examining the nature of the internal market and the type of contractual governance that is operating.

In essence, the dispute resolution system devised for the NHS ruled out recourse to the courts, and substituted an internal regime of conciliation and arbitration (Harden and Longley, 1995; Hughes, McHale and Griffiths, 1995, 1997). Guidance issued in 1991 anticipated two main classes of NHS contract disputes. Disputes over concluded contracts would be referred to an agreed arbitrator named in the contract, while those arising where contracts could not be agreed (because a party was acting unfairly) would be subject to mandatory conciliation by the RHA (or WO). In both situations, disputes that remained unresolved could be referred for a final decision to the secretary of state. Guidance indicated that this would normally mean a decision by an adjudicator selected from a centrally maintained panel of senior NHS managers.

Actually the DH has been reluctant to allow formal arbitration to be used, and has put considerable pressure on RHAs to deal with problems at local level. The message has gone out that purchasers and providers should settle problems bilaterally, and that – failing this – Regions should devise local mechanisms for dispute resolution. Recent research by Harden and Longley (1995) suggests a surprisingly diverse picture with some RHAs seeing their activity as conciliation, some as informal arbitration and some operating a two-staged process of conciliation followed by informal arbitration. In practice, the same mechanisms are applied to both pre-contract and contract disputes, though most coming through to RHAs are in the first category. English research by Appleby (1994) suggests that 30 per cent of DHAs and 20 per cent of providers surveyed were involved in (regional) arbitration in 1992/3, while Raftery, Mulligan, Forrest and Robinson (1994) put the figure for DHAs at 36 per cent in 1993/94.[8] At the time of writing no references to the secretary of state under the formal dispute resolution regulations had been made in England.

Our research revealed a similar picture in Wales, with WO taking the view that most cases could be settled by the parties themselves or by informal conciliation. With the exception of a few contracts for ambulance services, we found no examples of NHS contracts that named an arbitrator (as required by early guidance), and no indication that the 'agreed arbitration' route had been used. By September 1995, although WO had been informally involved in large numbers of contract wrangles in successive contracting rounds,[9] we could locate only five cases that had gone to conciliation and one to formal arbitration from our interviews.

These latter cases have all occurred since the start of the 1994/5 contracting round. Before then WO appears to have been reluctant to use the procedures laid out in official guidance, even though it intervened to deal with a small number of more intractable disputes. For example, one case that initially surfaced as a contract dispute between a HA and a trust attracted national publicity and eventually resulted in a major service review. Senior WO representatives met the parties and thrashed out an action plan, which, among other things, involved bringing in a neutral DGM to investigate the background to the dispute and injecting additional revenue. Here WO appears to have adopted a strategic management and financial control role, rather than the role of facilitation and neutral advice usually associated with conciliation.

Why did the formal procedure remain untried for more than three years? Socio-legal scholars have amply documented how alternative dispute resolution arrangements evolve in the shadow of formal legal processes, largely for reasons of cost and flexibility. But a situation where a formal, statutory procedure is supplanted by informal processes without ever having being activated would be virtually unique. What might explain the pressure exerted from the centre to avoid formal arbitration full stop?

When we interviewed senior civil servants in WO and the DH, they recalled worries that a proliferation of arbitration cases would be a costly exercise, and suggested that informal compromises would generally bring more enduring solutions. The advantages of informality may indeed have been important, but in this context informal settlement was not confined to the kind of bilateral negotiations common between private enterprises; rather, it involved a trilateral relationship, with WO exerting pressure on the contracting parties, within the overall hierarchical structure of NHS Wales. Dealing with disputes by

'banging heads together' (as one senior WO source termed it) or by devising more elaborate ad hoc forums for disputing parties to thrash out
problems has advantages in terms of low visibility and greater central
control.

Another factor is that the model of arbitration chosen for the NHS
would not have coped well with the types of disputes that were emerging. Harden and Longley (1995) found that most disputes coming
through to RHAs arose at the pre-contract stage, and this is also true in
Wales. Disagreements often centre on prices and activity levels for services not readily available elsewhere, and are often bound up with long-
standing issues of service re-structuring and finance. Consequently
many strategic planning issues, not resolved elsewhere, are washed up
on the shore of contracting. Arbitration, which essentially centres on an
authoritative judgement of principle, is unlikely to resolve these complex problems, which generally need to be addressed through management action and finding additional resources. The system used in the
NHS involves a pendulum decision, so that the adjudicator must find
for one side or the other and cannot compromise (DH, 1989b, para. 5.6).

Lon Fuller (1978), writing on the limits of adjudication, drew attention to the difficulties posed by 'polycentric' problems, where a change
to one element in a situation will have knock-on consequences elsewhere. A court of law is only able to consider certain aspects of the case
and the relevant legal rules, and its judgement may have complex and
unintended repercussions. Fuller cited disputes over resource allocation
as a classic example, and his analysis appears to apply to many NHS
contract cases. If a HA is instructed at arbitration to enter a contract at a
higher price than it had been willing to pay, the result may well be service reductions in areas not considered by the adjudicator. In situations
like this, informal negotiation, with the possibility of constructive
action to bring in more resources or agree other trade-offs, is likely to be
a more attractive option.

The first case to go to formal arbitration in October 1994 centred on a
contract between a DHA and trust signed under pressure against a time
deadline imposed by the WO. Precise information regarding transfers
of revenue from DHAs to new wave GPFHs is generally not available
until well into the financial year. To circumvent this problem it was
agreed that the final amount to be paid by the DHA to the trust would be
the sum specified in the contract less the value of the GPFH allocation.
The trust provided the DHA with data that it assumed would be used for

this purpose. The DHA, however, agreed revised figures with the fundholder that were used by the Welsh Office to determine the GPFH allocation. This change increased the GPFH's allocation and reduced the value of the DHA's contract with the trust. The DHA, which was a 'capitation loser' under the recently revised NHS resource allocation system, was unwilling to inject additional revenue to correct a shortfall that now appeared in the trust's budget and claimed that it had followed the proper procedure for calculating GPFH allocations. Conciliation failed to get either side to move and the case went to arbitration. Interestingly the WO (with the agreement of the parties) looked outside its pre-selected panel of senior NHS managers to nominate as adjudicator an academic with expert knowledge of the GP fundholder resource allocation mechanism. The adjudicator deemed that it was implicit that the contract between the DHA and trust would be based on the data supplied by the trust to be used in deriving the fundholder's allocation, unless the trust was told otherwise by the DHA. The trust claimed that the DHA did not inform the trust of the change in the value of the allocation, and the DHA was able to present no evidence that it had informed the trust. The adjudicator found for the trust and (in accord with the pendulum principle) required the HA to pay the contract sum claimed by the trust.

The similarities to, and differences from, arbitration in the private sector are instructive. As with most private arbitration there were issues of principle, centring here on the interpretation of rules for GPFH adjustments and whether too much revenue had been transferred from the DHA's budget (and contract) to GPFHs. However, the attention given to this internal NHS guidance may have moved the arbitration determination further from the terms of the contract than would have been likely in private arbitration. As in the Soviet example described earlier, there is a suspicion that administrative concerns (clarifying WO guidance to smooth a major service transition) and legal concerns (the contractual rights and obligations of the parties) are conflated. More fundamentally, the genesis of the dispute in the need to sign a contract in accord with the centrally-imposed NHS contract timetable, before essential financial information (provided by that same central department) was available, would be unknown in private sector contracting. The case is really only one step removed from the typical pre-contract dispute where parties who cannot agree price or activity, nevertheless find themselves constrained to enter a contract and seek third party assistance to find a way forward. Here an imposed timescale forces parties to sign a contract before basic issues of contract sum and volume of services purchased have been agreed, and the principle of contract as a freely-entered bargain is again violated.

The calculation of GPFH adjustments was a major issue in three of the conciliation cases mentioned above (one of which constituted the first stage of the arbitration case). The other conciliations related to a dispute over whether historical, base-funding levels for ambulance services understated provider costs, and one involving a secondary provider's attempts to re-structure costs, so that the aggreived trust's contract prices rose. All the cases are related to problems of adaptation and restructuring associated with development of the internal market. They do not involve disputes over performance or breach of contract (in terms of service volumes, quality or timing) of the kind common in the private sector. Though wrangles of this kind are not unknown in the NHS, our experience is that they are usually handled bilaterally at the time of annual re-negotiation of contracts. Action through the year tends to take the form of activating sanctions within the contract (penalty clauses) or direct management action by WO to insist that rules on matters like information returns and payment dates are complied with. Dispute settlement is thus a largely administrative process, bound up with the overall management of ongoing organisational change. Further weight to this interpretation is provided by recent changes in WO guidance, which allow officials to arbitrate directly on behalf of the Secretary of State where the value of the dispute is £20000 or less (DGM(95)7).

AN OVERVIEW

Data from Alpha district suggest that NHS contracting is a complex process that is difficult to match straightforwardly with any of the contract models identified in the academic literature. The hybrid market/ hierarchy arrangement of the reformed NHS has generated a range of hybrid contract forms. At the present time, the NHS environment remains a heavily regulated one and the closest parallels appear to be with the administered contract model. The handling of NHS contract disputes gives a particularly revealing indication of the importance of administrative, as opposed to quasi-legal processes. However, attempts to simulate features of market contracting mean that elements of other models are also discernible. Alpha represents a somewhat atypical case in that its adversarial approach incorporates more classical and neo-classical elements than we observed elsewhere, including, for example, detailed contract documents, clauses dealing with instalment payments, inspection visits and penalties, and close monitoring. However, some of these techniques have created problems and are being reconsidered as time goes by. Efforts were made to simplify contract documents, monitoring is proving to be a major resource-consuming activity, and some providers have succeeded in securing concessions on penalty clauses.

There were early predictions that NHS contracting might well evolve towards a relational form (Hughes, 1990; Hughes and Dingwall, 1990; Ranade *et al.*, 1992), and the research evidence suggests that some purchasers and providers have moved further down this route than Alpha, particularly in the area of community health services (Ferlie, 1992; 1994; Flynn *et al.*, 1995). Alpha remains strongly committed to detailed contract documents ('presentation'), but has moved some way from viewing contracts as discrete transactions, in which the best deal is won at all costs. Dealings with the main providers generally take a co-operative form, and we found many examples of extra-contractual understandings existing alongside the written contracts. Further movement towards a relational model would seem to imply greater flexibility in contract planning and drafting strategies. Currently there is a continued stress on presentation, partly linked to WO requirements for improved quality specifications, and very little appreciation that 'productive ambiguity' may have a role. Given the widespread planned use of contract variations, NHS purchasers and providers could certainly consider some of the technical drafting strategies for facilitating adjustments in long-term contracts reported in the relational contract literature (for example, Macneil, 1975).

To the extent that central intervention does not undercut the parties' sense of the importance of the bilateral relationship in the NHS contract, relational contract theory may have a continued relevance. One difficulty, however, lies in disentangling emerging perspectives on contracting from the influence of old administrative networks. Since 1948 the administrative segment of the NHS has had more of the character of a series of loosely linked networks than a fully integrated hierarchy. Co-ordination and co-operation between the various tiers – the central departments, the English regions, the DHAs and the Units has depended crucially on the quality of relationships between key players at each level. General management, planning, finance, medical and nursing staff typically developed overlapping networks through which information could be communicated and understandings could be reached. Often the smooth running of the organisation depended on informal arrangements which operated in parallel with formal planning and resource allocation processes. These arrangements have proved re- markably resistant to successive reform efforts, partly because the rela- tionships and the associated organisational cultures operated at a more fundamental level than the structural changes introduced to modify them.

The internal market poses a greater challenge to these established networks than any previous reform effort. Paradoxically, however, the development and regulation of the market in its first four years have depended on the very structures that it aimed to dismantle. As we have seen, old-style bureaucratic levers have been pressed into service to set the framework of rules within which contracts operate, and many of the informal backstage activities undertaken to support the system rely on established administrative networks. Some of the relational elements in contracting behaviour that we observed arise from the continued influ- ence of the old order. With time these may well develop to resemble the co-operative behaviour common in private business, but there is also the possibility that they represent the 'absorption' of the reforms into the old NHS order.

At the time of writing, the direction of change is difficult to predict. After a period when politicians, managers and policy analysts con- stantly talked of the need to let the internal market 'settle', it is becom- ing apparent that the present system is in far from stable equilibrium. The move towards 'a primary care led NHS', and the next general elec- tion are two immediate factors likely to ensure that the service remains in flux. In the meantime, there are revealing indications (from the Healthcare 2000 Inquiry and elsewhere) that some senior figures asso- ciated with the NHS reforms all along saw them as a transitional arrangement. A move towards privatisation, probably through a steady drift to pluralism rather than simple ownership transfer, now seems a real possibility.[10] The influence of the Private Finance Initiative in stimulating investment on NHS sites, more NHS work for private pro- viders, and the growth of parallel non-NHS provision for the better off, would all have an impact on contracting practice. The number of conventional, legally-binding contracts between commissioners and private providers would grow to become a more significant part of overall contract portfolios. If NHS contracts covered sub-contracted services using private facilities on NHS sites, their form would need to be reviewed to take account of indemnity and other issues. Against this background of the blurring of the boundaries between public and private domains, NHS and market contracts may yet come to resemble each other more closely.

Notes

1.   As well as conventional market regulation we are now seeing the creation of planned markets and associated systems of contracting (Saltman and von Otter, 1992), which seem even more clearly in tension with the classical model. Hayek's (1978) discussion of Mandeville's *Fable of the Bees* is perhaps the classic exposition of the liberal view that markets evolve spontaneously from human interaction, rather than as a result of deliberate planning or the imposition of economic structures on one class by another.

2.   It is significant that a large proportion of the disputes handled by State Arbitrazh were 'pre-contract' disputes about the terms of a contract under negotiation, rather than the non-performance of a concluded contract (see also Kroll, 1986).

3.   Hayek (1978, 303–4) describes contracts in the planned economy as a 'self-contradictory approach', which poses two major difficulties. First, public ownership tends to prevent competition dictating how much capital each enterprise shall have and what risks it shall run, and second, Government faces the dilemma that, if it lets the market work, it can do nothing to ensure that the resultant distribution of resources between enterprises corresponds to a distribution it regards as socially just. These are essentially the same criticisms that contemporary new right theorists make of public sector quasi-markets.

4.   In contrast to typical contracts for waiting list initiative work, the relationship with this provider was seen as an ongoing one and indeed the contract was renewed in 1995/6.

5.   As part of the Patient's Charter initiative the Government has required HAs to enforce standards in twenty-two key areas, covering areas such as waiting times, cancellations of surgery, use of named nurses, discharges, ambulance response times, information given to patients and complaints procedures.

6.   Some clauses relating to larger penalties specify that, where the cost of treating waiting list patients elsewhere exceeds the penalty, full costs

must be met by the provider. In technical legal terms these may lie in a grey area between penalties and agreed damages.

7. In Wales, DGM(91) 39 and in England, EL(91) 11.
8. Both studies are surprisingly imprecise about the processes to which the figures refer, but it appears that they relate to informal regional arbitration (with the possibility, given the mixed pattern found by Harden and Longley (1995), that some conciliation cases were also counted). Our own information from senior NHSE sources is clear that, by September 1995, the formal NHS dispute resolution procedure had not been used in England and all 'arbitration' to date had been carried out at regional level.
9. It is difficult to be precise about the figure. Welsh Office sources suggest they advise or instruct on 'three or four cases a month' involving disputes'. In our interviews with finance officers/contracts managers in Welsh DHAs and NHSTs, we were advised of 34 instances where WO had been involved in disputes in 1994/5, but several respondents indicated that they would not necessarily be aware of all such communications, particularly at chief executive level.
10. The parallels with the civil service, the original site for experiments in 'management in government' later applied to the NHS, are difficult to escape. At the time of writing, a large number of Next Steps Agencies, whose future – at the time of creation – was said to lie firmly in the public sector, are being prepared for privatisation.

References

Allen, P. (1995) 'Contracts in the National Health Service Internal Market', *Modern Law Review*, 50, 321–42.

Appleby, J. (1994) *Developing Contracting: A National Survey of District Health Authorities, Boards and Trusts*, Research Paper 15 (Birmingham: National Association of Health Authorities and Trusts).

Atiyah, P.S. (1995) *Introduction to the Law of Contracts* (5th edn) (Oxford: Clarendon Press).

Berman, H.J. (1963) *Justice in the USSR* (New York: Vintage Books).

Campbell, D. and D. Harris, (1993) 'Flexibility in long-term contractual relationships: the role of cooperation', *Journal of Law and Society*, 20, pp. 166–91.

Cohen, A. (1994) 'Managers, markets, contracts and professionals', in J. Carrier and P. Owens (eds) *Interprofessional Issues in Health and Community Care* (London: Macmillian).

Daintith, T. (1986) 'The Design and Performance of Long-Term Contracts', in Daintith, T. and G. Teubner (eds) *Contract and Organisation: Legal Analysis in the Light of Economic and Social Theory* (New York: de Gruyer).

Dawson, D. (1994) 'Costs and Prices in the Internal Market: Markets v the NHS Management Executive Guidelines', *CEH Discussion Paper 115* (York, University of York: Centre for Health Economics).

Department of Health (DH) (1989a) *Working for Patients*. Cmmd 555 (London: HMSO).

Department of Health (DH) (1989b) *Contracts for Health Services: Operational Principles* (London: HMSO).

Department of Health (DH) (1990) *Contracts for Health Services: Operating Contracts* (London: HMSO).

Ferlie, E. (1992) 'The creation and evolution of quasi-markets in the public sector: a problem for strategic management', *Strategic Management Journal*, 13, 79–97.

Ferlie, E. (1994) 'The creation and evolution of quasi-markets in the public sector', *Policy and Politics*, 22, 105–12.

Flynn, R., S. Pickard and G. Williams (1995) 'Contracts and the Quasi-market in community health services', *Journal of Social Policy* 24, 529–50.

Friedman, L. (1965) *Contract Law in America: A Social and Economic Case Study* (Wisconsin: University of Wisconsin Press).

Freidmann, W. (1975) *Law in a Changing Society*. (3rd edn.) (London: Stevens and Son).

Fuller, L. (1978) 'The forms and limits of adjudication', *Harvard Law Review* 92, 352–409.

Harden, I. (1992) *The Contracting State* (Buckingham: Open University Press).

Harden, I. and D. Longley (1995) 'NHS Contracts', in Birds, J., J. Bradgate and C. Villiers (eds) *The Termination of Contracts* (London: Chancery).

Harrison, A. (1993) 'Introduction', in A. Harrison (ed.) *From Hierarchy to Contract, Reshaping the Public Sector*, Volume 7 (Oxford: Policy Journals/ Transaction Books).

Hayek, F. (1978) *New Studies in Politics, Philosophy and the History of Ideas* (London: Routledge and Kegan Paul).

Hazard, J.N. (1969) *Communists and their Law* (Chicago: University of Chicago Press).

Hudson, B. (1994) *Making Sense of Markets in Health and Social Care* (Sunderland: Business Education Publishers).

Hughes, D. (1990) 'Same story, different words', *The Health Service Journal*, 100, 5193, 423–4 (22 March).

Hughes, D. (1991) 'The reorganisation of the NHS: the rhetoric and reality of the internal market', *The Modern Law Review*, vol. 54, 88–103.

Hughes, D. and R. Dingwall (1990) 'Sir Henry Maine, Joseph Stalin and the reorganisation of the National Health Service', *Journal of Social Welfare Law*, 5, 296–309.

Hughes, D., J.V. McHale and L. Griffiths (1995) 'Contract disputes, whose problem?', *The Health Service Journal*, 105, 5449 (April 20), 18–20.

Hughes, D., J.V. McHale and L. Griffiths (1997) 'Settling contract disputes in the National Health Service: formal and informal pathways' in Flynn, R. and G. Williams (eds) *Contracting for Health: Quasi-markets in the NHS* (Oxford: Oxford University Press).

Jacob, J. (1991) 'Doctors go to hospital', *Public Law*, Summer, 255–81.

Kroll, H. (1986) 'Decentralization and the precontract dispute in Soviet industry', *Soviet Economy*, 2, 51–71.

Kroll, H. (1987) 'Breach of Contract in the Soviet Economy', *Journal of Legal Studies*, 16, 119–48.

Laughlin, R., J. Broadbent and H. Willig-Atherton (1994) 'Recent financial and administrative changes in GP practices in the UK', *Accounting, Auditing and Accountability Journal* 7, 96–124.

Le Grand, J. and W. Bartlett (eds) (1993) *Quasi-Markets and Social Policy*, (London: Macmillan).

Loeber, D.A. (1964) 'Plan and contract performance in Soviet Law', *University of Illinois Law Forum*, 128 (Special Issue: *Law in Soviet Society*, ed. W. R. LaFave) 138–9.

Longley, D. (1990) 'Diagnostic dilemmas: accountability in the National Health Service', *Public Law*, Winter, 527–52.

Macneil, I.R. (1975) 'A primer of contract planning', *Southern California Law Review* 48, 627–704.

Macneil, I.R. (1978) 'Contracts: adjustment of long-term economic relations under classical, neo-classical and relational contract law', *Northwestern University Law Review*, 72, 854–905.

Mawhinney, B. (1993) *Purchasing for Health: A Framework for Action* (Leeds: NHSME).

Pomorski, S. (1977) 'State arbitrazh in the USSR: development, functions, organisation', *Rutgers Camden Law Journal*, 9, 61–115.

Posner, R.A. (1969) 'Natural monopoly and its regulation', *Stanford Law Review*, 21, 548–643.

Raftery, J. and G. Gibson (1994) 'Perspectives on purchasing: banking on knowledge', *The Health Service Journal*, 104, 5389, 28–30.

Raftery, J., J.A. Mulligan, S. Forrest and R. Robinson (1994) *Third National Review of Contracting 1994/95* (Leeds: NHS Executive Purchasing Unit).

Ranade, W. *et al.* (1992) *Perspectives on the Market: NAHAT Project Paper 6* (Birmingham: National Association of Health Authorities and Trusts).

Saltman, R. and C. von Otter (1992) *Planned Markets and Public Competition* (Buckingham: Open University Press).

Speer, B.M. (1971) 'Contract rights and the planned economy: peaceful co-existence under the 1969 Soviet statues on deliveries of goods', *Law and Policy in International Business*, 3, 510–41.

Tam, H. (1994) *Marketing, Competition and the Public Sector: Key Trends and Issues* (London: Longman).

Welsh Office (WO) NHS Directorate (1992) *Caring for the Future: The Pathfinder* (Cardiff: Welsh Office).

Williamson, O.E. (1979) 'Transaction-cost economics: the governance of relations, *Journal of Law and Economics*, 22, 233–61.

Williamson, O.E. (1981) 'Contract analysis: the transaction cost approach' in P. Burrows and C. Veljanovski (eds) *The Economic Approach to the Law* (London: Butterworths).

Vickers, J. and G. Yarrow (1989) *Privatization: An Economic Analysis* (Cambridge: Mass., MIT Press).

Vincent-Jones, P. (1994a) 'The limits of contractual order in public sector con-
    tracting', *Legal Studies* 14, 364–92.
Vincent-Jones, P. (1994b) 'The limits of near-contractual governance: local
    authority internal trading under CCT', *Journal of Law and Society*, 21,
    214–37.

5 Specialist Health Services within the New NHS

Penelope M. Mullen

INTRODUCTION

Problems have long been associated with the provision of specialist health services, including securing equity in access, ensuring adequate provision and the financial viability of providers, developing new services and avoiding unnecessary service duplication. However, the introduction of the internal market within the NHS has raised additional concerns. Providers of specialist services are experiencing problems in contracting with multiple purchasers, and purchasers have been faced with unpredictable high-cost extra-contractual referrals (ECRs). The change towards capitation funding is moving funds away from districts with specialist providers and the reorganisation of health services within London and other major cities threatens the very existence of some hospitals providing specialist services (Tomlinson, 1992; Thompson, 1993). Reports by specialist committees have highlighted actual and potential problems for specialist services within the new contracting environment and have drawn attention to the need for appropriate contractual arrangements (CSAG, 1993; BPA, 1993).

SPECIALIST HEALTH SERVICES

Specialist health services are characterised by low volumes (arising from the rarity of the conditions they treat), high costs and/or the need for scarce specialised skills. Thus they must, or should, be delivered to populations larger than those of Health Authorities (HAs) or health commissions. As well as economies of scale resulting from more intensive use of high-cost capital equipment and staff, there is often a clinical need for a 'critical mass' of cases in order to maintain the expertise of clinical teams and to secure improved clinical outcomes.

Catchment populations for different specialist services vary from national down to sub-regional. Determining appropriate catchment population sizes requires detailed clinical, economic and social analysis, with the different criteria often in conflict. The clinical case will depend on studies of outcome such as Heinemann *et al.* (1989), clinical consensus and expert opinion. Clinical outcomes must be balanced against any additional costs associated with specialist treatments to ensure provision is cost-effective. Economies of scale and the need for a 'critical mass' of patients must be weighed against access to services.

An important related question is the size of the 'commissioning' population necessary to carry the financial risk associated with high-cost specialist care, where low volumes result in very large fluctuations in demand/need. Over the range of specialist care, HA or health commission populations should be sufficiently large to carry the combined financial risk. However, problems could occur with devolved purchasing to smaller populations, and with rigid allocations of funds to specific services or care groups.

Access and non-financial barriers to specialist services

The choice of evaluation criteria does, of course, depend on the value system adopted. Assuming the adoption of an 'Egalitarian Viewpoint', as developed by Williams (1990), access to specialist services should be determined solely by need and every patient should receive treatment and care at the specialist level, and from the specialist service, appropriate to their condition.

Access may be affected by inadequate supply caused by under-funding, poor distribution leading to unequal provision, as well as organisational and fiscal barriers. However, even where adequate services are available and no financial obstacles or perverse incentives exist, there may be under-referral to, under-use of, or unequal access to, specialist services.

One cause is referring doctors' inadequate knowledge of what is clinically possible. The Clinical Standards Advisory Group (CSAG) Report discusses this in respect of Adult Cystic Fibrosis and Childhood Leukaemia (CSAG, 1993). Mihill (1993) also reports complaints by specialists and researchers of the failure of doctors to refer patients to specialist centres. Reporting their study on acceptance for treatment of End-Stage Renal Failure (ESRF), which showed that GPs and non-renal consultant physicians rejected a significantly higher number of cases than did nephrologists, Challah *et al.* (1984) suggest that under-referral contributed to the low acceptance rate of dialysis and transplantation within the UK. This problem is not, however, confined to specialist tertiary care. Goldberg and Jackson (1992) report under-referral by GPs to specialist mental health services, and Chamberlain and Tennant (1991) suggest that there is under-referral to rheumatological services. In both cases, lack of knowledge by GPs of what specialist services can offer is cited as a possible reason.

A second cause is geographical remoteness. Various studies, for example that by Dalziel and Garrett (1987) on acceptance and treatment rates for ESRF, have shown that population usage rates of health facilities vary in inverse proportion to the distance from those facilities.

Specialist services in the 'old' NHS

Prior to 1991, funds for hospital services were passed from the Department of Health (DoH) to Regional Health Authorities (RHAs), largely on a capitation basis. Regions, in turn, funded District Health Authorities (DHAs), normally on a capitation basis, adjusted for cross-boundary flows and historical service patterns. The cross-boundary-flow adjustment was based on specialty-specific mean costs-per-case applied to historic cross-boundary flows. DHAs then passed on funds, usually cash limited, to the hospitals under their control. In principle, patients from any District could be treated in hospitals located in any other District.

Designated national or supra-regional services were funded nationally, along with post-graduate teaching hospitals which also deliver very specialised services. However, most specialist services were run by the DHAs within whose boundaries they were sited. Districts were financed for such services by a mixture of explicit national or regional top-slicing, cross-boundary-flow adjustments and/or historic funding. That hybrid system led to considerable debate. DHAs with specialist services complained that they were under-compensated for the additional costs, whilst DHAs without such services complained of being financially penalised to pay for services within other Districts. Problems of expenditure control, equity and sensitivity to national and local priorities also arose (Mullen, 1986).

Specialist services in the 'new' NHS

In the new NHS, funding is still passed from the DoH to RHAs on a weighted capitation basis. HAs receive their funding from RHAs, increasingly also on a capitation basis, with some of that funding being allocated directly to GP Fund-holders (GPFHs) to pay for a range of elective in-patient care, out-patient visits and community services for their own patients. Hospitals and other providers gain their income by selling services to purchasers (HAs and GPFHs), either through contracts, or as one-off extra-contractual referrals (ECRs). In general, patients may now only be treated at any particular hospital, either if that hospital holds a contract with their home HA or GPFH for that service, or if their HA or GPFH agrees to pay on an individual ECR basis. However, HAs are required to pay for emergency ECRs.

Official guidance on specialist services and tertiary referrals

Guidance on specialist services and on the funding of tertiary referrals (i.e., referrals made by a medically qualified consultant to another medically qualified consultant) has been issued on several occasions since the publication of *Working for Patients* (DoH, 1989a). Whilst not all tertiary referrals are to specialist services, most referrals to specialist services are tertiary referrals and thus their funding will have considerable impact on the provision of, and access to, specialist services.

Guidance on specialist services

Early advice suggested that existing designated supra-regional services would continue to receive direct funding from the Centre for their fixed costs, but that variable costs would be met by GPs or DHAs under contract (DoH, 1989b); this was later modified to the proposition 'that a proportion of the costs (not necessarily defined as the fixed costs) would be met centrally and the balance locally' (DoH, 1989c). Both documents suggested that decisions on the organisation of regional and multi-district services should be taken locally. Conceding that, initially, a Regional role, using the funding model proposed for supra-regional services, may be desirable, both documents go on to stress a 'presumption in favour of contract funding'.

Later, following concern 'about the funding of small specialised units offering services to multiple purchasers' (DoH, 1992c), the NHS Management Executive initiated a study to 'identify the scope of this problem, the funding arrangements in place for these services, and possible alternative means of funding or contracting for these services' (NHSME, 1993a). At the same time RHAs were required for 1993–4 'in liaison with purchasing authorities, to ensure that appropriate contracting arrangements are in place for the purchasing of specialised services'.

Contracting for Specialised Services – a Practical Guide, which resulted from that study, lists principles for 'good practice' in contracting for specialist services including: using contracts rather than relying on ECRs or cost-per-case for low volume services; employing sophisticated contracts and avoiding simple block contracts; structuring contracts to accommodate unpredictability or variance in demand; and entering into longer 'fixed term' contracts or 'rolling' contracts (NHSME 1993b; DoH, 1993c).

The Guide describes methods of contracting for specialist services (RHA Purchasing; Regionwide Purchasing; Consortia Contracts; Co-ordinated Contracts; Individual Contracts; Sub-contracting), which have been adopted in different parts of England. However, when drawing up a list of recommended arrangements, RHA purchasing is omitted as 'it removes from local purchasers the key responsibility of assessing the needs of their local population and ensuring appropriate provision of services to meet these needs' (NHSME, 1993b, para. 4.18). Further, because of insufficient population bases and lack of information, contracts between specialist providers and individual DHAs are not recommended unless they evolve from multiple purchasing arrangements. RHAs 'in liaison with purchasers and providers of specialised services' are charged with ensuring that these recommended 'arrangements are used for the purchasing of specialised services as appropriate' (NHSME, 1993b, para. 4.22).

'Lead-purchasing' – an arrangement where 'one purchaser acts on behalf of a number of other co-purchasers' – is also encouraged. The main roles of the 'lead-purchaser' are seen as Advice, Contract Negotiations, Monitoring and Networking (NHSME, 1993b, pp. 23–9). Under 'lead-purchasing' co-purchasers may each have their own contract with a specialist provider but, where there are 'multiple purchaser contractual arrangements', the 'participating purchasers must agree the basis for calculation of their relative shares to the contract. This will vary dependent on the circumstances of individual services but may include historical usage, planned usage, weighted population shares or some hybrid of these' (NHSME, 1993b, p. 3).

Guidance on tertiary referrals

According to early advice 'the costs of tertiary referrals would be met by the referring hospital' (DoH, 1989b), arguing that for reasons of patient management it would be more efficient 'for the unit which receives the initial referral to subcontract directly for "follow on" work' (DoH, 1990a). As an alternative approach, it was suggested that DHAs contract directly with the receiving providers for tertiary referrals.

However, the high information demands of sub-contracting were later recognised and, because 'NHS information systems are generally not at present sufficiently sophisticated for units to be able to identify and price the likely incidence of tertiary referrals separately from other referrals', for the medium term it was suggested that DHAs contract directly with providers of tertiary referral services (DoH, 1990b).

Where tertiary referrals were not covered by a contract, ECR rules applied (i.e. requiring prior authorisation from home DHAs for non-emergency ECRs, but DHAs having to pay for emergency ECRs) (DoH, 1990c). It was later stressed, however, that 'it is important to remember that for tertiary referrals, the patient has already started NHS treatment and therefore has a legitimate expectation that it will be completed' (DoH, 1992a).

Following a review it was ruled that 'from 1 April 1993 providers in England will no longer be required to obtain prior authorisation from the appropriate purchasing authority or GP fund-holder before accepting tertiary referral patients' (DoH, 1992b). Purchasers must simply be informed of such cases and they 'will be expected to meet the cost of treatment in the same way as is already the case for emergency extra-contractual referrals'. Responding to concern about the potential for 'cost shifting' between provider units, further guidance goes on to stress that 'consultants are expected to make responsible use of the new scheme', they should refer within contracts where possible and have readily available lists of specialties and units with which the purchasing authority already has contracts. In addition, in the case of long-term and high-cost referrals, 'consultants should be able to justify such a referral in terms of value-for-money'. The guidance further states that 'Purchasing authorities remain responsible for defining priorities and communicating them to consultants' (DoH, 1993a). It was later reported that 'these new arrangements have eased some of the problems that specialised provider units were experiencing in obtaining authorisation for tertiary ECR referrals from purchasing authorities' (NHSME, 1993b).

EXPERIENCE IN PRACTICE

As noted above, the new funding and contracting system within the NHS brought increasing concern about the fate of specialist services (Forsythe, 1993; Duley 1993; CSAG 1993; Donaldson 1992). In the early years the effects were mitigated as many regional and multi-district services continued to receive top-sliced funding, and designated Supra-Regional services continued to be centrally fully funded and thus provided 'free' to the patient's DHA (SRSAG, 1992). However, specialist services are now being required to move into the new 'internal market', HA allocations are moving from historic funding towards capitation funding (DoH, 1993b) and there is official encouragement to move from 'block' to 'cost-and-volume' and 'cost-per-case' contracts (DoH, 1992c).

Along with the continuation of top-sliced funding, several RHAs developed new arrangements including lead purchasing and region-wide purchasing (NHSME, 1993a). However, even in the early years much contracting for specialist services took place at district level. For instance, the CSAG Committee found the predominant contracting arrangement for 1992/3 was 'purchasing fully devolved to DHAs' for the four specialist services under investigation (CSAG, 1993). Both sub-contracting and direct contracting are found amongst contracts for specialist services and tertiary referrals.

Provider viability, especially difficulties faced by small specialist units dealing with large numbers of purchasers, has been a major cause of concern. This situation leads to volatile funding for specialist units and threatens their survival. However, as Donaldson (1992) points out, in theory there should be no difficulty. Purchasers are responsible for assessing and meeting the needs of their populations and their decisions 'should enable people with clinical need who require services not available in a local hospital to receive them'. Thus the market will ensure sufficient provision. But, Donaldson continues, assessment of need for specialist services is not simple and is subject to multiple influences. Further, providers of specialist services fear purchasers may lack specialist medical advice and may not recognise *bona fide* need. For instance, the CSAG working group on cystic fibrosis found that 'many purchasers had no knowledge of what should be purchased' (CSAG, 1993). On the other hand, allowing the level of use and provision of specialist services to be provider-led undermines the purchasers' role in determining and meeting the needs of their population.

If purchasers have financial incentives to procure care at an inappropriate specialist level, appropriate use of specialist services may be frustrated. The British Paediatric Association Working Party received a number of reports 'of a reluctance to make appropriate referrals of critically ill children to PICUs (Paediatric Intensive Care Units) because of the potential financial cost to the referring district of extra-contractual referrals' (BPA, 1993). Whilst there is considerable scope for clinical (and possibly social) argument about the appropriate specialist level for any particular form of treatment, there are fears that purchasers may put pressure on non-specialist providers to take on care more appropriate to specialist centres. For instance, having stated that 'in our view larger centres generally offer greater technical competence and the highest chance of successful therapy' for childhood leukaemia, the CSAG Report continues that some 'shared-care clinicians mentioned the possibility of pressure on them from local managers to increase their level of care and refer only extraordinary problems to major collaborative centres' (CSAG, 1993). Further, 'entrepreneurial providers ... may be tempted to offer a service', which might lead to the proliferation of small centres.

Problems also arise where purchasers pay for fewer procedures than the specialists deem clinically necessary. Not only can this increase waiting time, but it can distort clinical priorities since 'access [to CABGs] depends on contracted activity rather than clinical priority' (CSAG, 1993).

Similar problems arise if providers have financial disincentives to making appropriate referrals – a particular risk with 'sub-contracting', where the initial provider is contracted to pay the tertiary provider for tertiary referrals. A recent report suggests that some neonatal intensive-care cases are being inappropriately treated at non-specialist centres and that the financing arrangements may be contributing to a reluctance to make appropriate tertiary referrals (Lewis, 1993).

At the same time, there is evidence of provider resistance to the inclusion of low-volume, high-cost services within block contracts. For instance, Moore (1992) reported several hospitals deciding to charge for neonatal intensive care on an ECR basis, instead of including it in block contracts for maternity services.

Although these factors could contribute to a reduction in the viability of specialist services, at the same time it should be recognised that many, especially those working at the non-tertiary level, suspect that there is a tendency to high-cost, non-efficient empire building on the part of those involved in specialist services.

POSSIBLE MODELS FOR CONTRACTING FOR SPECIALIST SERVICES

Drawing on the ten contracting models considered within the Northern RHA (Donaldson, 1992), the NHSME's (1993a) recommendations, and arrangements observed in practice, the following methods of funding specialist services are identified:

- **Top slicing** where funds are top-sliced, nationally or regionally, before allocations are made to HAs. All residents of the top-sliced authorities would have access to the services without further charge to their home authority, but the imputed contribution made by any individual authority need bear no relation to the use made of those services by the residents of that authority.
- **Subscription, insurance or consortia** where HAs combine (voluntarily or compulsorily) to pay, in advance, subscriptions or 'insurance premiums' to finance specialist services. As above, all residents would have access to the services without further charge to their home authority. Subscriptions could be capitation or usage based. Similarly, insurance premiums could be community or risk rated.
- **Emergency or tertiary ECRs** where the HA (or GPFH) is compelled to pay for its residents treated outside contracts, but has no control over whether or not that treatment is given.
- **Contracts:**
  a) **Sub-contracts** where the purchaser places contracts with the initial provider for both secondary and tertiary referrals, and that

provider sub-contracts with tertiary providers for 'follow on' tertiary referrals.

b) **Block contracts** where each purchasing authority places a contract with each specialist provider to supply specialist services to the purchaser's residents as required.

c) **Cost-and-volume contracts** where each purchasing authority (DHA) places a contract with each specialist provider to supply a pre-determined volume of specialist services to the purchaser's residents.

(Any of the above contract arrangements could be negotiated in conjunction with lead purchasing systems.)

- **Elective ECRs** where the purchasing authority (DHA) decides on a case-by-case basis on whether to purchase specialist care outside a contract.

Evaluation of the funding methods

Combining an equity criterion with efficiency-based criteria and new concerns brought about by the NHS changes – sensitivity to purchaser priority and ensuring provider viability – the following criteria for evaluating contracting arrangements for specialist services within the new NHS are suggested:

- Equity
- Sensitivity to DHA Priorities
- DHA Expenditure: Degree of Control and Predictability of Level
- Provider Viability
- Potential for Adequate Supply
- Potential for prevention of duplication and over-supply
- Appropriateness of referrals and use:
  a) No (financial) incentive for inappropriate referrals (which would lead to over-referral/use)
  b) No (financial) disincentive to appropriate referrals (which would lead to under-referral/use)

An evaluation of the different funding methods listed above against these criteria is given in the Table. This indicates that whilst no funding method scores well on all criteria, some methods do appear better than others. Without weighting the individual criteria it is not possible to identify the best alternative but, as well as the selection of the evaluation criteria being value-laden, any such weighting of the criteria must also be value-laden.

Alternative methodologies

The above methodologies are not, of course, exhaustive. Two radically different approaches are discussed below.

Provider subsidy

The provision of a direct, but partial, subsidy to specialist services to cover their 'excess costs' might remove incentives to purchase care at an inappropriate level. Such a subsidy should make the referral decision financially neutral, i.e. the price-per-case charged by a specialist unit would be similar to the price charged by a non-specialist unit for the same specialty or treatment group. Since purchasers would have no financial incentive to favour one provider over another, decisions should be made on purely clinical criteria. However, care must be taken to ensure that the 'excess costs' are justified by the nature of the services and do not result from inefficiency. Such a 'provider subsidy' should be in addition to compensation for excess service costs associated directly with teaching and/or research (Tomlinson, 1992, para. 163).

DHA 'Top-slicing' or pre-allocation

Although HA populations should be sufficiently large to carry the financial risk over the range of high-cost specialist care, within each general specialty area high-cost specialist treatments will be competing with far larger numbers of lower-cost treatments. On the analogy of GP fund-holding, which effectively constitutes a pre-allocation or top-slicing for elective surgery, it would be possible to establish a 'top-slicing' system for specialist services at HA level. A proportion of each HA's budget would be (compulsorily!) earmarked for regional, supraregional and other designated tertiary services. HAs would use these earmarked funds to pay for specialist treatment on an ECR or contractual basis. Thus expensive, low-volume services would be competing against each other, and not against primary and secondary care services. Such a system would reduce HA autonomy in choosing how much to allocate to specialist services, but HAs would retain the power

Table 5.1 Evaluation of possible funding methods for specialist services within the new NHS

Funding methods	Potential for equity	Sensitivity to DHA priorities	DHA expenditure control level	Predict-ability	Potential provider viability	Potential for ensuring adequate provision	Potential for avoiding duplication	Appropriateness of referral/access	
								Potential over-referral	Potential under-referral
Top slicing	High	Low	Low	High	High	High	High	High	Low
Subscription/insurance or consortia	High	Low (unless considerable individual DHA influence)	Low	High	High	High	High	High	Low
Emergency or tertiary ECRs	High	Low	Low	Low	Medium	High	Low	High	Low

C O Sub-contracts with initial providers	Low	Depends on incentives to initial provider	High	High	Low*	Fairly low*	Low*	Low	High
N T R Block contracts with tertiary providers	Low	High	High	High	Medium*	Medium*	Low*	High within contract	Low within contract
A C T S Cost-&-volume contracts with tertiary providers	Low	High	High	High, up to contract limit	Fairly low*	Fairly low*	Low	High, up to contract limit	Low up to contract limit, high beyond
Elective ECRs	Low	High	High	Medium	Low	Low	Low	Low	High

* 'Scores' may be higher where lead purchasing arrangements are in operation.

to impose priorities between specialist services. Providers of specialist services would, collectively, have an assured income, but individually funding may still be volatile. Deciding how much should be 'top-sliced' or pre-empted for purchasing specialist services would be no easier, but no more difficult, than determining GPFH allocations for elective care. Like the GPFH scheme, this system would constrain a DHA's ability to pursue its own priorities.

CONFLICTS WITHIN THE NEW NHS

The debate on specialised services throws into sharp relief some of the conflicts within the new NHS, which arise, to a large extent, from the attempt to introduce a competitive market model into a health system which largely retains the values of a socialised health service.

As noted above, dealing with large numbers of purchasers leads to volatile funding for specialist units and threatens their survival. But the logic of the internal market is that the pattern of specialist service provision will be determined by the decisions of purchasers. However, it is worth noting that most countries, even those where the provision of health care is largely market-based, have introduced some form of regulation to ensure the viability of specialist providers, to equalise geographical distribution and to avoid unnecessary duplication. The London reviews further demonstrate the difficulties of leaving the pattern of specialist provision to the market – to the aggregated purchasing decisions of individual HAs.

However, any central planning of the provision of specialist services risks over-riding DHA priorities. There is clearly a conflict here. In ensuring 'that appropriate contracting arrangements are in place for the purchasing of Specialised Services' (NHSME, 1993a), it is not clear whether RHAs, in addition to ensuring security of funding for specialist units, were required to ensure that the priorities of the individual DHAs are respected or were required to ensure equity of access for all residents. The former is more consistent with the philosophy of the new NHS, but could result in intentional geographical inequity in access to specialist services. The latter would over-ride local priorities and distort the internal market.

Likewise systems, such as the 'provider subsidy', which introduce fiscal neutrality into decisions on referral to, and use of, specialist services, could be argued to violate a principle of the new NHS, i.e. that cost/finance should be taken into account in purchasing decisions. On the other hand, it would be difficult to argue in favour of financial arrangements which encouraged clinically inappropriate care and treatment.

Denial of access and political visibility

The effects of denying access to specialist services depend on the type of service. Specialist care can be classified into: a) care and treatment which can *only* be provided by specialist centres (e.g. heart transplants, neurosurgery); and b) care and treatment which *can* be provided at non-specialist or less-specialised centres, although it may be inadvisable, clinically, so to do (e.g. neonatal intensive care, neonatal surgery, treatment of severe head and spinal cord injuries, management of adult cystic fibrosis). Where an HA fails to purchase a treatment under category a) its residents will simply not receive that treatment at all. For high profile services, this may become headline news fairly quickly and be subjected to the type of debate raised by other explicit rationing decisions within the NHS. However, failure to purchase treatment under category b) may mean that treatment is still provided, albeit inappropriately, by a less specialised centre. The problem could thus remain hidden. Potentially, however, treatment being delivered at an inappropriately low level could prove an even more intractable problem than the more clear-cut total denial of access to treatment.

The new rules on tertiary ECRs complicate the above analysis. It is likely that many cases requiring time-limited 'one-off' treatment will, or could, reach specialist units as tertiary referrals, possibly overriding the priorities of the home DHA. However, where treatment or care can be supplied by a less-specialist unit, and especially where continuing care is required, the tertiary ECR loophole may be less apparent.

The future of the regional role

The discussion above suggests that under devolved market-based healthcare systems, the organisation and funding of specialist services require intervention by organisations covering larger populations than those of HAs. The NHSME Guide recognises this since, although considering RHA purchasing 'not appropriate for the purchasing of these services', it does envisage a major role for RHAs in connection with the funding and provision of specialist services (NHSME, 1993b). Further, as well as requiring RHAs 'to ensure that appropriate contracting arrangements are in place for the purchasing of specialised services' (NHSME, 1993a), the Guide requires RHAs, in their role as 'market managers', 'to review those services which warrant explicit contractual attention as specialised services' (NHSME, 1993b). RHAs are also required to: give support to 'lead purchasers'; ensure, together with purchasers and providers, 'that appropriate specialised medical and clinical advice is available'; determine, with purchasers, 'the appropriate population size or base for the "sensible" contracting of specialised services'; and ensure, in consultation with NHSME Outposts, 'that contracting arrangements between purchasers and providers include explicit arrangements to consider the funding of developments including "pump-priming"' (NHSME, 1993b).

The Guide envisages a major role for RHAs in the development of existing services and introduction of new services and treatments, and recommends that 'top-slicing' should continue as an intermediate approach to the issue of funding innovations (NHSME, 1993b). Some form of regional role is also envisaged in the related areas of medical education and research and development.

However, the government abolished RHAs in early 1996, having reduced their number from 14 to eight in April 1994 (DoH, 1993d). 'Those functions of the RHAs which remain the responsibility of central management' will be taken on by eight new NHS Executive regional offices, which will *inter alia* be responsible for ensuring that purchasers have continued access to development activities which aim to increase their effectiveness in areas such as purchasing highly specialised services' (DoH, 1993d). Whilst it is too early to determine how, and to what extent, the former RHA role in respect of specialist services will be continued by the new NHS Executive regional offices, a less pro-active role might be inferred from the statement that the existing outposts of the NHSE 'have been commended for their "light touch" approach and the regional offices will build on this' (DoH, 1993d). This would be consistent since, as noted above, a strong regional role is incompatible with the stated philosophy of the new NHS.

CONCLUDING REMARKS

There is no easy solution to the question of the organisation and funding of specialist services. There are conflicting objectives, not least the question of equity versus local priorities. In addition, specialist services usually require some form of centralised planning or control which conflicts with the market ethos and devolution of decision-making.

Problems of conflict between financial incentives and appropriate levels of treatment are not, however, confined to the Health Service. Social Services Departments face similar problems in connection with access to specialist drug and alcohol treatment units. As in the NHS, there are legitimate arguments about the efficiency and appropriateness of referrals to such units rather than to less specialised care. However, where there are clear financial incentives to approve treatment at a less specialised level, it may prove difficult to convince everyone that decisions have been made on purely 'clinical' grounds.

Many aspects of the organisation of specialised services will be determined by clinical imperative as well as clinical opinion. However, the clinical aspects will always have to be tempered by questions of geographical access and economics. Whilst there is legitimate clinical argument about the efficacy of specialist services in individual cases, the problem of inappropriate substitution of services at a lower level may prove to be more important, although less politically visible, than the more dramatic problem of total denial of access to specialist services.

The most appropriate form of organisation and funding methodology for specialised services will ultimately depend on the value system which encompasses the health service as a whole. There is widespread agreement that any market within the NHS must be a 'managed market'. The question, in respect of specialised services, is exactly where that 'managed market' will finally be located in the spectrum between a pure market-based system and a planned system.

References

BPA (1993) *The Care of Critically Ill Children*, Report of a Multidisciplinary Working Party (London: British Paediatric Association).

Chamberlain, M.A., and A. Tennant (1991) 'Health Service Reforms and Access to Specialist Services', *British Journal of Rheumatology*, 30, 322–4.

Challah, S., A.J. Wing, R. Bauer, R.W. Morris and S.A. Schroeder (1984) 'Negative selection of patients for dialysis and transplantation in the United Kingdom', *British Medical Journal*, 288, 1119–22.

CSAG (1993) *Access to and Availability of Specialist Services*, Clinical Standards Advisory Service (London: HMSO).

Dalziel, M., and C. Garrett (1987) 'Intraregional variation in treatment of end stage renal failure', *British Medical Journal*, 294, 1382–3.

DoH (1989a) *Working for Patients*, White Paper CM555 (London: HMSO).

DoH (1989b) *Funding and Contracts for Hospital Services*, Working for Patients Working Paper 2 (London: HMSO).

DoH (1989c) *Contracts for Health Services: Operational Principles* issued under EL(89)MB/169 (Department of Health).

DoH (1990a) *Contracts for Health Services: Operating Contracts*, issued under EL(90)MB/24 (Department of Health).

DoH (1990b) *Contracting for Tertiary Referrals*, EL(90)194 (Department of Health).

DoH (1990c) *Charging for Extra-Contractual Referrals*, FDL(90)7 (Department of Health).

DoH (1992a) *Guidance on Extra Contractual Referrals*, issued under EL(92)60 (Department of Health).

DoH (1992b) *Tertiary Referrals*, EL(92)97 (Leeds: Department of Health).

DoH (1992c) *Review of Contracting – guidance for the 1993–94 contracting cycle*, (Leeds: Department of Health).

DoH (1993a) *Guidance on Operation of Notification Arrangements for Tertiary Extra-contractual Referrals*, HSG(93)8 (Leeds: Department of Health).

DoH (1993b) *Progress towards Weighted Capitation*, FDL(93)20 (Leeds: Department of Health).

DoH (1993c) *Contracting for Specialised Services*, EL(93)98 (Leeds: Department of Health).

DoH (1993d) *Managing the New NHS* (London: Department of Health).

Donaldson, L.J. (1992) 'Maintaining excellence: the preservation and development of specialised services', *British Medical Journal*, 305, 1280–4.

Duley, J.A. (1993) 'No charge for unique service', *British Medical Journal*, 306, 1543.

Forsythe, M. (1993) 'Commissioning specialist services', *British Medical Journal*, 306, 872–3.

Goldberg, D. and G. Jackson (1992) 'Interface between primary care and specialist mental health care', *British Journal of General Practice*, 42, 267–9.

Heinemann, A.W., G.M. Yarkony, E.J. Roth, L. Lovell, B. Hamilton, K. Ginsberg, J.T. Brown and P.R. Meyer (1989) 'Functional outcome following spinal cord injury', *Archives of Neurology*, 46, 1098–102.

Lewis, P. (1993) 'Cash crisis puts babies' lives at risk', *The Observer*, 29 August 1993.

Mihill, C. (1993) 'Doctors "fail to refer cancer patients to specialist centres"', *The Guardian* 1 December 1993.

Moore, W. (1992) 'Health chiefs fear crisis over neonatal ECR bills', *Health Service Journal*, 102, 4.

Mullen, P.M. (1986) 'Funding of Supra-Authority Services', *Public Money*, 6, 55–8.

NHSME (1993a) *Good Practice and Innovation in Contracting* (Leeds: NHS Management Executive).

NHSME (1993b) *Contracting for Specialised Services – A Practical Guide*, issued under EL(93)98 (Leeds: NHS Management Executive).

SRSAG (1992) *Annual Report for the period ending 31 March 1992* (London: Supra Regional Services Advisory Group).

Thompson, M. (1993) *Review of the Research and Development Taking Place in the London Postgraduate Special Health Authorities*, A Report by the Review Advisory Committee (London: HMSO).

Tomlinson, B. (1992) *Report of the Inquiry into London's Health Service, Medical Education and Research* (London: HMSO).

Williams, A. (1990) 'Ethics, Clinical Freedom and the Doctors' Role', in A.J. Culyer, A. Maynard and J.W. Posnett (eds), *Competition in Health Care: Reforming the NHS* (London: Macmillan).

6 Doctors in Management

Annabelle Mark

Developing doctors as managers successfully depends on understanding what differences and similarities there are between management and medicine. As a first step in bringing them together some agreement is needed on a shared value system (Mark, 1995). Medicine has an explicit value system and code of ethics still largely based on the Hippocratic oath and its modern equivalents; managers however have only lately attempted to structure a value system (IHSM, 1994) in common with the more general thrust in society towards establishing an ethical basis to managerial activities. The difference between these two sets of values, and the feared erosion of medical power and values by management (White, 1993), has been the foundation of much of the conflict which has existed so far between management and medicine and is also in part responsible for the latest review of core values in medicine (BMA, 1995).

At its most extreme medicine has taken a very negative and somewhat pejorative view of the role of management, exemplified by Tony Hicklin's (HSJ, 1992) statement:

> Management is the syphilis of the NHS. Doctors usually acquire it in unguarded moments. It is much more pleasurable than work, but produces illusions of grandeur.

However, key changes now require managers to ensure that doctors take a more active role in managing the organisation. As a first step to reviewing the success of this change, an evaluation of the national programme of training for doctors in this new role has provided some insight into the process so far (DoH/NHSME, 1993; Mark, 1994a). Necessarily, however, it cannot encompass the significant developments of doctors as managers of General Practice fundholding organisations, where the most significant intra- rather than inter-professional shifts in power have taken place as a consequence of the reforms (Abel-Smith, 1992).

Evaluation of training and its outcomes in the short term is itself problematic (Mark, 1993), but it is susceptible to a qualitative approach informed by a connoisseurship (Turner, 1988) and expertise (Glaser and Chi, 1988) in both management training and the National Health Service. These perspectives then rest upon Kirkpatrick's (1960) four levels of training evaluation, which are:

• How did participants react?
• What did participants learn?
• How did participation change behaviour?
• What organisational goals were affected?

BACKGROUND

The recent reform of health care in the UK directly influenced a policy objective of long standing in the National Health Service, that is, to involve hospital-based doctors in the management process or – to put it in Mackenzie's (1979) terms – to ensure that power and responsibility rest in the same place. The history of such attempts to involve hospital doctors in the management process have achieved varying degrees of success with the different approaches which have been employed, for example the development of Cogwheel in the 1960s (Ministry of Health, 1967), consensus management (DHSS, 1974) in the 1970s, and the Resource Management Initiatives (DHSS 1986) of the 1980s, but it would seem that no significant changes in medical culture, despite the arrival of general management (Hunter and Williamson, 1989), had been discernable as a result of any of these strategies (Harrison *et al.*, 1993). The introduction of hospital Trusts (DHSS, 1989) once again thrust the issue into the spotlight by giving hospitals the duty to demonstrate the involvement of the doctors in the management process as a prerequisite for reaching the mirage of autonomy which Trust status promised. The search was on for a new but understandable model to achieve this, which had both political and organisational credibility. As with many policy initiatives of the Thatcher years (Amidon, 1994), it was not surprisingly an American concept, that of the Clinical Directorate model as demonstrated at the Johns Hopkins (New England Journal of Medicine, 1984), which was hijacked into the UK on the back of this concorde for change.

A consequence of this new organisational structure, together with the new culture implied by internal markets brought about by the latest reforms (DHSS, 1989), was the identification of a need for some formal training and its subsequent evaluation (Lorbieki *et al.*, 1992; DoH/ NHSME, 1993) for this new hybrid of the doctor/manager as Clinical Director. The Department of Health decided on pump-priming investment for this training but set out quite specific criteria about the type of training it perceived as necessary (NHSTD, 1991). This training entailed the exclusive use of business school courses where it was assumed the proper lessons of management, not distorted by the special pleadings of the health sector, could be learnt. The focus of attention was on organisational needs rather then on the personal training needs of the doctors (DoH/NHSME, 1993) and it exemplifies a key conundrum which still remains. How are organisational needs and personal needs appropriately integrated to provide the best solution for both? Evaluation of both the pilot sites (Lorbiecki *et al.*, 1992) and the cross-Regional investment are complete (DoH/NHSME, 1993; Mark, 1994). They have revealed that training has secured a reduction in perceived stress for those juggling the dual activities of managerial and clinical work, which incidentally may be facilitating improved performance in both the practice of management *and* medicine by those who have received it. It thus provides some hope that such dual roles are manageable for individuals, as well as providing a necessary bridge to future organisational success (Maxwell, 1993). Nevertheless problems remained. For example:

• Women doctors had to contend with a glass ceiling which was differentially double- and even sometimes triple-glazed by medical, managerial and sometimes academic career ladders (Mark, 1991a; Mark, 1993a), although once the medical ceiling had been broken by the attainment of consultant status there was some evidence, at least in the London Special Health Authorities, that the ratio of women doctor/managers was moving towards a third of participants (Mark, 1994), which is more in keeping with the managerial path ratio. This perhaps shows that women doctors recognise that the most open root for further career progress is often management, rather than the medical or academic career ladders, and/or that they are more appropriate to the task than their male colleagues (Kolb, 1992).

- Team development (Thompson, 1993) was not being addressed adequately and this was reflected in the funding of management training to separate professional programmes like the doctors.
- Finally, succession planning occured by default rather than design (Tremblay, 1993; Mark, 1993a; Mark 1994), not least because the future into which participants will succeed is so unknown or uncertain.

In addition, with the subsequent structural change bringing about the removal of Regional Health Authorities in 1996 (DoH, 1993), the presence of leadership and the momentum needed for carrying forward the initiative from initial enthusiasts, likely to be at most a normal distribution of 25 per cent of doctors, to the main body of the profession is questionable. The leadership became dislocated between the Trusts and the vacuum which in 1994 existed above them (DoH, 1993), in spite of the statements of intent for the future set out following the Functions and Manpower Review (NHSE, 1994). Developments in the role of postgraduate medical deans, and locally based education and training consortia still leave the future in some doubt for this hybrid between the two. What the NHS now requires is some assurance that the doctor manager is a viable, recognisable and sustainable feature of the new NHS, and the evaluations of management training have at least provided the basis to answer some key questions to identify this. These are:

- Can doctors become managers?
- Have changes in knowledge skills and attitudes occurred?
- How long will it take?
- Who should be involved and where?
- Are there any costs as well as benefits to the change?

CAN DOCTORS BECOME MANAGERS?

The transition from the role of the doctor, focusing primarily on the individual's needs, to the manager who focuses on organisational needs had already been attempted in a variety of structural ways before the changes set out in 1989 (DHSS, 1989) were proposed. However, rather than concentrating again on design and structure via Cogwheel or the Resource Management Initiative, it is perhaps more useful to look at what work doctors actually do, to see what managerial activity is revealed. In common with reviews of other health workers, like nurses (Gibbs *et al.*, 1991), the origins of this change are more evident if hospital doctors are not viewed so much as a homogeneous group but rather as possessing at least two distinct sets of skills or activities within the organisation. The first set of what may be called primary interface activities is traditionally seen in the hands of the surgeons and physicians, and involves the use of expert knowledge and opinion in the diagnosis of illness and the allocation of treatment for the individual; this activity is the one upon which the nebulous notion of clinical freedom, or the right to unmanaged status, is founded (Hoffenberg, 1986). The second set of activities, which substantially supports the first, involves the control and delivery of diagnostic and therapeutic intervention using expert skills and knowledge, as demonstrated most obviously by pathologists, anaesthetists and radiologists. There is of course an interchange between the groups and activities, so, for example, we see anaesthetists cornering the allocation of treatment for pain control; but the broad division is supported by the separation of the latter group into what are termed the support specialities. This increasing fragmentation (Turner, 1995) of the profession based on task differentiation was recently used to political advantage in attempts to reform American health care (Iglehart, 1994), and seems set to continue and develop, as for example, surgeons become more specialised in increasingly specific parts of the body, for example hand surgery.

It is within the second set of activities, the support specialities, that the management of the network of the organisation's activities has become apparent, and it is not therefore surprising that a high proportion of those interested in gaining management knowledge and skills should have come from these specialities (Lorbiecki *et al.*, 1992; Newman and Cowling, 1993) which already operate in something of a dependency relationship to the primary interface activities. This professional separation of the differing activities has implications for the structural shape of the organisation, what Clinical Directorates there should be, and who should undertake the leadership of them. This last issue identifies an important problem, which is, that without sufficient participation in leading Clinical Directorates from those doctors undertaking the primary interface activities described above, the doctor/manager will not make the necessary impact on the profession as a whole, and the medical profession's participation in management will be open to question in the longer term. Doctors can acquire the skills and knowledge of management but in the words of one participant doctor (DoH/NHSME, 1993) 'management training may well persuade me that it is something in which I do not wish to be involved', especially where what is experienced is the conflict which will arise for doctor/managers when they fully appreciate that the choices of one role can represent the demands and constraints of another (Stewart 1983). Fully appreciating the nature of the tasks that managers have to do may however, as the HAS (1992) suggested, enable those relinquishing the activity to others to provide them with more meaningful expert support from their own domain (Mark, 1993).

The second issue which needs to be addressed is, where are medical managers' roles located in management, and why (Mark, 1991). Management wishes to see them often tackling the operational issues (DoH/NHSME, 1993); this indicates an assumption of increasing managerial control (Edmonstone and Havergal, 1995) which may not be sustainable (Harrison and Pollitt, 1994). The doctor/managers' view is often to give the operational work to the business manager, which leaves them to tackle the strategic roles. This is much in line with Handy's (1984) interpretation of professional cultures, but perhaps contrary to the dominant (Mintzberg, 1988) operating mode of medicine with its emphasis on logic and analysis; it also contrasts with the more intuitive and creative approach required for strategy development (Mintzberg, 1994). The role may be a mixture of both, but the questions remain: what is the most appropriate set of priorities for the doctor/managers, given the limitations on their time when undertaking the dual doctor/manager role; and what training needs are implied by this?

Some answers to these questions may lie in what we know about the career paths of hospital doctors and managers. The former are characterised by very rapid movement between, and thus little allegiance to, organisations until consultant status is reached, when they often remain within one organisation until the end of their working life of 20 to 25 years. In contrast, managers are characterised by continual movement due to organisational and personal development needs, although this has slowed somewhat in recent years at senior levels due to recession and the flatter organisations now in place. It would seem therefore, that the strategic role for doctors on reaching consultant status is not only personally and professionally desirable, but also, given their longer-term commitment to one organisation under current career paths, it may also be the most appropriate and sustainable if the 'us and them' culture, as Best (1993) has suggested, is to be thrown overboard. These career differentials also continue to be reinforced by fixed-term contracts for managers, which have further constrained their ability to feel a long-term commitment to one organisation. Furthermore, the question of who will shape the strategic future contains within it the role of influencing not only the activity but also the perception of the organisation. This perspective demonstrates a requirement for doctors once again to exercise power both overtly and covertly within the organisation, by participating in *all* of Lukes's (1974) three modes: not only to modify the conduct of others in observable conflicts (managing conflict), nor just to determine what gets on the agenda (influencing), but also to shape the preferences and cognitions of others (managing perceptions) or – as the Chief Medical Officer recently put it – to 'set the vision' (IHSM, 1994a) to go in the appropriate strategic direction.

In this way it is possible to see how the doctors are thus able to move back into the driving seat which managers and the age of managerialism have attempted to remove them from; it also helps to explain why propositions for the future (Harrison and Pollitt, 1994) moderation of the rise of managerialism from the political domain (Mark and Scott, 1992) seem so convincing. The regular political ritual of manager bashing can be undertaken with even greater impunity if the culture and strategic direction are in the hands of others, namely doctors.

HAVE CHANGES IN KNOWLEDGE, SKILLS AND ATTITUDES OCCURRED?

The anticipated changes in knowledge and skills were assumed to be the need for a more businesslike approach by doctors to the management of the health resource, which is why doctors were seen to need immersion in the business school sector (NHSTD, 1991). This was inappropriate in many instances, as the managers with equivalent organisational status attending programmes in business schools were well in advance of the doctors' knowledge base in the managerial domain. They were seen as somewhat threatening to a high-status group of professionals who did not want to expose their lack of knowledge in such an environment. Those who did benefit in the national programme from such courses were those who had already had substantial training in management within their own Regional peer group programmes, but such local programmes were not always available, and may continue to be given low priority by Postgraduate Medical Deans, who will almost exclusively control the future training agenda for doctors. Training failures identified in the national evaluation (DoH/NHSME, 1993) support the need for initial training within the safety of a peer group, as the evolution identified inadequate preparation in inappropriate contexts as one of the negative factors leading to poor training outcomes for those who did not benefit from the national programme. The type of skills and knowledge training needs identified by the doctors further confirms this point. Their initial concerns centre around skills such as IT, finance, time management, and face-to-face management. Only later, when such skills have been acquired, are they able to look at the broader picture of the more creative activity of strategy development in a multiprofessional team context. The high levels of stress which both Ham and Hunter (1988) and Burgogyne and Lorbiecki (1993) had identified as a major problem for the doctor/manager were somewhat ameliorated by management training (DoH/NHSME, 1993). However this might be as much because, as research has implied (Newman and Cowling, 1993), it provides know-how to subvert the management or political agenda, as it is about the acquisition of skills and knowledge of managerial 'thought styles' (Dopson, 1993) in the psychological group (Huczynski and Buchanan, 1991) of management. Attitudinal change is the hardest to interpret although a transfer from a positivist, or ostensibly objective, approach to a more phenomenological or subjectively influenced appreciation (Mark, 1993) of management is one indicator that they have moved away from the more simplistic notions of management as just a set of techniques (Fitzgerald and Sturt, 1992). In addition repeated acknowledgement of powerful role models in the managerial domain (DoH/NHSME, 1993) confirmed this as one of the most influential learning experiences when combined with the formal training progamme, especially if such role models could also act as mentors.

These findings are perhaps not surprising when set in the context of doctors' formative training and socialisation in medicine, which also relies on such dysfunctional (McKegney, 1989) methods and fits with the concept of a power-orientated culture (Pheysey, 1993), to which medicine as a profession still adheres. Management meanwhile has attempted to define the organisation as moving from a role to an achievement culture (Pheysey, 1993), as one of the significant shifts which have occurred within the NHS culture in recent years (HAS 1992).

HOW LONG WILL IT TAKE?

There is a difference between what the organisation requires of doctors and what it requires of managers and this is reflected in the educational and socialisation process for doctors within the hospital. While there are many convincing arguments that doctors are *de facto* managers within their own jobs, the training needs identified by the doctors in the management training initiatives (Lorbiecki *et al.*, 1992; DoH/NHSME, 1993) are evidence that while they may (Spurgeon, 1993), or may not (Audit Commission, 1995) use them they are not currently *taught* the skills and perhaps, as Griffiths had suggested (May, 1993), they should be, as part of both their undergraduate and postgraduate professional training. The Middlesex University evaluation (DoH/NHSME, 1993) used the technique of self-efficacy (see note 1, p. 123) to determine if a positive correlation existed between training and individuals' improved ability to perform managerial tasks. The evidence was conclusive in identifying that training not only improved the individual doctor's perceived ability, but that a direct link existed between the number of days training which were provided and the increase in self efficacy or perceived ability to complete tasks. The implications for improving training are compelling for doctors and managers themselves, as it may also indicate something already well recognised in the nursing sector (Hancock, 1993), which is that by providing training a higher quality service can be achieved without necessarily increasing overall labour costs. It is also evident that management training will only succeed if it is provided at the appropriate point in the individual's development in a personal *and* organisational context (Mark, 1991) otherwise it will be wasted, and may even cause negative feedback within the organisation (DoH/NHSME, 1993). Recent reviews of medical training (Working Paper 10, Calman, 1993) at least now have such information to assist with decisions about the future shape of medical training for those who will have to function effectively as doctors and managers in the organisation of health care in the UK.

Identifying training needs is only one part of a complex equation which will also include some identification of the positive and negative factors which can contribute to an individual doctor's willingness to become involved in management. The most pressing incentive for both individual doctors and the medical profession is to continue to maintain control over their own working environment. However each individual experiences a unique combination of factors, both personal and organisational, which influence their inclination to consider managerial roles. These factors have been identified as follows:

RECEPTIVENESS FACTORS FOR DOCTORS GOING INTO THE MANAGEMENT ROLE

	Personal		*Organisational*
• age, sex and ethnicity	P		
• personality	P		
• medical speciality	P	and	O
• stage of organisational development			O
• stage of organisational change in culture			O
• stage of individual development	P		
• peer pressure			O
• experience as both observer of and participant in management	P	and	O
• training	P	and	O
• negative pressure – i.e., non-participation in management will result in loss of control in the professional domain			O
• loss of private practice income	P		

Further work is required here, perhaps using some measure for each factor then aggregating the total; this could help not only to predict the likely number of potential doctor/managers at any one time in an organisation, but also to facilitate the gaps identified in developing tools to encourage proactive succession planning (Spurgeon, 1993; DoH/NHSME, 1993) for this role. Such information could also inform future training and development needs for those only just entering medical school, especially if measures are based on self perception. So, for example, a question would be asked about what difference individuals see their sex making to their ability not just to perform a management role but also to gain access to it. Use of the factors in this way has much in common with the basis of self-efficacy (Lane, 1992) as used in the Middlesex evaluation. The alternative approach would need to utilise a notional ideal type of organisation, training or set of experiences, which is not a productive approach because of the variety of routes to success, and future organisational types. The question thus changes from how long will it take, to how much investment and change to the training of doctors in the process of management is likely to be available and acceptable, especially given the predicted shortfall of doctors to provide the medical services required from them in the next 10 to 20 years (DoH, 1992). A secondary but not insignificant factor which influences all of this is the receptiveness of managers to the doctor/manager role when it is seen as an inappropriate use of medical time or, worse still, a threat to lay managers' own career paths (Mark, 1991). As Sutherst and Glascott (1994) put it, 'Close rapport with the Chief Executive via whom you can make your position clear is valuable. You will have to learn how to continue to be influential in a managerial system which may not like doctors to be influential.'

WHO SHOULD BE INVOLVED IN THESE ACTIVITIES ?

This question has two separate aspects to it. These are:

• Who should be provided with training?
• Who should be involved in developing and providing the training?

The first question is one that individual organisations will have the answer to, based on some of the criteria already outlined above; but in defining needs, individual Trusts may not have a sufficient critical mass to acquire appropriate training for themselves. Collaboration is required between Trusts but this will require considerable ongoing support and encouragement from the Regional Office of the Management Executive (NHSE, 1994)in the face of the competitive advantage that such training might give. The alternative to this is the use of pre-packaged external courses, but where these do not fit the *personal* as well as *organisational* needs there is the danger of some negative feedback if individual clinicians are not adequately prepared; this again seems more likely in the absence of coherent activities across all professional groups in providing for both personal and organisational development.

The other issue highlighted in the research was the encouraging outcome of action learning (Revans, 1980) sets for groups of doctors (DoH/NHSME, 1993). Where there were logistical problems, and a lack of adequate facilitation at the outset, there were some failures in the use of these sets. However, the benefits which did accrue occurred for the most part where doctors from different Trusts and units were able to exchange ideas and experiences across separate organisational cultures without fear of reprisal. Sharing problems in this way may be contrary to the spirit of competition in the internal market, but it is more successful in developing the doctor/manager than learning sets which are developed within the same unit. It also prepares these doctors for the richness of differences they will experience when they become part of inter-disciplinary teams where true action learning can take place. The use of the doctor/manager learning pairs as developed in the Yorkshire Region (Tietjen, 1991) also had advantages in overcoming tension between doctors and managers which had already been identified as existing between Chief Executives and Clinical Directors (Thompson, 1993). Problems with learning sets occurred where units operated in relative geographical isolation, but the benefits were often also severely disrupted by the rapid changeover in managers as part of their career progression into other organisations, thus further emphasising the continual dislocation and change in setting strategy and operationalising it within the management domain. The last seemingly obvious points are :

* doctors need to have a management task to do once they have received training (Smith, 1992), otherwise they experience frustration at not being able to apply their learning;
* their attitudinal changes must be supported by changes in structure and practice once back in the workplace (Holloway, 1991);
* the organisation eventually has to manage those doctors who feel a sense of powerlessness when their role as Clinical Director ceases or moves on to others, otherwise the experience of loss, demonstrated in any change process, may result in disaffection and disruption by what can be described as the loose cannon factor. One solution to this would be a more systematic use of these post-management doctors in

a management-training role for other doctors in their organisation, as befits the original seedcorn intentions of the Department of Health management training programme (DoH/NHSME, 1993).

WHO SHOULD BE INVOLVED IN DEVELOPING AND PROVIDING THE TRAINING?

In addition to the local role of doctors training doctors, as just suggested, there are many other players with an interest in developing and providing training, but the policy implementation lessons of the evaluation are that what was assumed to be the best option by Ministers, that of business schools, would, if adopted without amendment, have had many negative outcomes, and that sensitivity to local culture and organisational development is critical in identifying appropriate training (DoH/NHSME, 1993). Given the changing status of Regions during this time and the centralisation of their role (DoH, 1993), such interpretation and adaptation may not be a feature of the future, and implementation will suffer as a consequence.

The individual units and Trusts, the profession and its representatives (like the GMC, the BMA, the Royal Colleges, the British Postgraduate Medical Federation, the NHSE), and the suppliers, be they Business Schools, in-house trainers or consultants – all have a role to play in both the provision and recognition of management training (Tremblay, 1993), but it is the necessary co-ordination of these groups on behalf of those needing the training which gives rise to concerns now. Without such co-ordination the best will continue to train and the worst will be set up to fail (MacLachlan, 1992) with all that is implied in this for an increasingly mobile workforce. Attention must also focus on the parallel progress in experience, and training and development agendas (Tremblay, 1993), because where training has facilitated experience, progress has been greater than where training has not been reinforced by doing, as Smith (1992) had already suggested after the pilot phase. The last and perhaps most significant issue is the adequate evaluation of training to ensure that individual and organisational needs are both met; such future evaluation must take both the long- as well as short-term perspective, if research outcomes are not to be subject to the limitations which using only short-term approaches can be prone to.

WHAT ARE THE COSTS OF THE DOCTOR/MANAGER ROLE?

The costs of the doctor/manager role can be separated into costs to the individual, costs to the team/organisation, and costs to the profession.

Costs to the individual

Personal problems for individuals have been associated with:

- *role stress*: especially ROLE OVERLOAD in attempting to maintain clinical activity to an unreasonable degree while undertaking the management role, and secondly ROLE AMBIGUITY, which occurs because of a lack of knowledge and skills, combined with inappropriate attitudes to the task of management;
- professional and, consequent upon this, social *isolation*. This will depend on both the ratio of clinical versus managerial involvement together with the degree of organisational development within directorates and trusts;
- *loss* of professional personal development activities, for example, research and development in the doctor's own clinical speciality.

There are also costs which occur at both an individual and organisational level and these have been defined (Mark, 1993a) as:

Costs of the transition to doctor/manager

- *colleague credibility* – or the need to retain clinical work, or have a high personal reputation in clinical activities, if participation in the managerial role is to be worthwhile for the individual *and* the organisation.
- *management credence* – or the implied degree of belief in the importance of an activity, namely management, from which professional (e.g., doctor) participation can be withdrawn when issues become too difficult, or professional medical career paths once again take precedence.
- *lay management marginality* – or the threat to lay management careers inherent in doctors undertaking the management role.
- *manpower misappropriation* – or the costs to patients of appointing doctors who on balance are good managers rather than doctors who are good clinicians. Such casualties are already a feature of the edu-

cation sector where similar decentralisation of management to professionals has also occurred (Gretton, 1994).

* *interpretive adaptability* – or the cost to organisations of the mobility of managers, and increasingly doctors, who move between health care organisations and have to adapt to the increasingly varied interpretations of management and the managerial role.

This mobility is likely to grow within the medical profession because of new career paths following the implementation of Calman (1993) and an increased specialisation which will push some doctors towards a proliferation of cross-organisational working as knowledge-based networkers (Quinn, 1992). This is already a fundamental feature of the Special Health Authorities, where such issues adversely affect, amongst other things, succession planning in the Clinical Director role (Mark, 1994a). It may also prevent doctors from full participation in a strategic management role for any one of the organisations in which they will undertake professional work.

Costs to the team/organisation

Within the organisation, where doctor/managers operate largely as leaders of a team, there are significant problems associated with transposed clinical teams and inter-professional rivalries. Problems of team development have occurred partly because the culture of the clinical team was assumed to be automatically available for transposition to a managerial culture, often without adequate team training. In addition, within the team the tensions created by the new hierarchy, which is presented by the doctor/manager role are exacerbated. The result of this is a rivalry which is symptomatic of:

* the pre-existing rivalry between professional groups;
* the marginalisation of some of these groups in favour of doctors undertaking the management task;
* the disempowerment of these groups with the removal of functional and professional accountability;
* the failure by most training providers at the time of the research to develop adequate strategies for integrating personal and organisational development of these management directorate teams, rather than just the individuals within them.

Some solutions to these problems are available in the form of new organisational formats (Harrison and Pollitt, 1994), for example outsourcing (Mark, 1994b), where separate specialised organisations are set up to provide a uniquely developed set of core intellectual and service capabilities important to customers; such solutions may be particularly important for the somewhat disempowered professions allied to medicine (Spurgeon, 1993). Other groups are also adopting strategies to cope, for example the transfer of some nurses into the business manager role, and more generally the review of career paths (IHSM Consultants, 1994) implied by the new roles which cross all professional groups and in time may lead us to a new climbing-frame metaphor (Charlwood 1994), more appropriate to the flatter achievement-based culture.

Costs to the profession

The cost to the profession of medicine in the new doctor/manager role may not be as great as it at first seems, if it enables them to maintain their hold on power while adding to their sense of corporate responsibility. What must be evaluated is the proportion of medical time which will be taken up in the organisational rather than individual management process. If this factor reduces excess supply in times of medical manpower over-provision it will have served a purpose, but is it the right one, and can the role be sustained in times of medical manpower shortage?

CONCLUSION

In summary therefore, in answer to the questions we first set out with, we can conclude as follows:

- *Can doctors become managers?* Yes, but only if the right doctors are involved to undertake the appropriate tasks for the organisation and its future. This will involve not just the avoidance of sabotage but positive support from this expert domain (Mark, 1993).
- *Have changes in knowledge, skills, and attitudes occurred?* Changes have occurred in all areas where the right personal and organisational context for learning has been provided. These are both skill-based in areas such as Information Technology, finance, time management

and face to face management, and knowledge-based within a developing understanding of themselves and the groups and organisations with which they are working. Attitudinal changes from a mindset based on the rational objective perception to a more intuitive subjective and creative approach has also happened in the most advanced participants.

- *How long will it take?* A long time, but it can be influenced by the amount of investment in training and the use of relevant personal and organisational development techniques at all stages of the doctor's career.
- *Who should be involved in these activities?* Individually those who want it, organisationally all those using doctors as managers, through a co-ordinated but locally sensitive approach by those with vested interests in making it work.
- *Are there any costs as well as benefits to the change?* There are costs not previously acknowledged, but which require ongoing support from the profession and the organisation if doctors are not to be dissuaded from participating. In addition, the effects on other professional groups of the doctor/manager role can no longer be ignored if the team approach to health care is to be sustained. Finally doctors need management training to improve their own professional culture and to develop the efficient and effective delivery of medical care (Audit Commission, 1995).

Formulating the future

In general terms it is difficult as yet to discern real and consistent trends because of the variables at work across the UK at both an individual and organisational level. Such variety is encouraging if it indicates a willingness not to attempt to find a one-best-way to develop doctor/managers. The concern, however, must also be that such short-term adaptations as have been studied so far may have further backlashes or side effects (Burgogyne and Lorbiecki, 1993) than those already identified above. Questions which remain yet to be answered are:

- Is the doctor manager a desirable role?
- Will it be sustained?
- If so in whose interests?
- Are there any realistic alternatives and if so what are they?

These questions all contain within them two key conundrums: what difference has it made, and what has made the difference? The first is, as Lukes (1986) suggests, an interest in the outcomes of changing the power relationships in the organisation, and the second is an interest in identifying the new locus of that power. In answering the first it has to be said that there may have been an initial error of judgement in focusing on the doctor/manager as a solution to the problems of managing health care. This is in part because the team of other professionals involved could become isolated from the managerial and clinical agendas of health care if they feel they are unable to influence either the managerial or professional domain (Mark and Scott, 1992), now that they are joined together in this way. The alternative suggestion – that the model of doctors involved in management can only be sustained if 'conflict between medical need and available resource can be dealt with elsewhere in the system' (Burgogyne and Lorbiecki, 1993) – misses the point of the development entirely. The overriding purpose of this initiative was to address the need to combine the power to allocate resources (the doctor's traditional role) with the responsibility for their fair distribution across varying interest groups served by the organisation (the manager's traditional role), thus encapsulating within the doctor/manager role the conflict which exists between these separate interests. However if, as Pascale (1990) suggests, 'there are some tensions in organisations which should never be resolved once and for all as contention across boundaries is not only inescapable but can be productive', then the doctor/manager role may prove a negative suppressant of that tension (Mark and Scott, 1992) which would otherwise thrust the organisation forward, implying perhaps a covert strategy of restraint.

Disentangling the positive and negative effects of the various aspects of the reforms can confuse the issue, so, for example, successful working with others because of the purchaser/provider split must not be mistaken for the positive development of doctor/managers, especially as outstanding examples of the genre often rest for their success on charisma or, in French and Raven's (1958) terms, referent power, which is not sustainable in the long term. Incentives for continued and developing involvement of doctors in management may however be sustained because the doctor/manager role has moved the medical profession into new sources of power within the organisation. Not only do they have access to expert power (French and Raven, 1958) which is traditionally associated with the professions, they also have access to legitimate or position power within the management of the organisation. This gives greater access to new levers which govern the exercise of both reward power and coercive power through budgets, human resource management and performance-related pay differentials. However, as Huczynski and Buchanan (1991) point out, while it is possible to operate from multiple sources of power, the use of one type of power often affects the ability to use another source. Thus the use of position power can reduce the ability to exercise expert power when conflicts in the two roles arise for the doctor/manager.

Furthermore, the exercise of all types of power occurs through a social process which requires the acceptance of leaders by followers, who can thus be willingly led; as Mole and Dawson (1993) point out, the legitimacy of the clinical director and thus the doctor/manager role rests on their acceptance by peers *and* other health professionals.

Lastly, both academic analysis (Jefferys, 1991) and managerial action, in reviewing skill mix and reprofiling the workforce, point towards the relationships *between* professional groups and, in instances like management and medicine, their potential for merger (Ranade, 1994). This may well prove to be the more appropriate starting point for the future evaluation of the health care reforms in the 1990s rather than a continued focus on separate professional groups (Calman 1993; DoH, 1994), even when they have been forced or even shoved (Dopson, 1993) across operational domains.

What does seem likely is that there may be a better understanding of management, even without direct participation in it, by a growing number of doctors. This will make Tony Hicklin's 1992 statement – which metaphorically uses syphillis, a disease which has also undergone significant historical and social transformation – seem increasingly outmoded.

Note 1

Self-efficacy. This is a measure which individuals have of their confidence in being able to undertake a task or master a situation successfully, and has a higher validity than psychometric testing of personality.

The concept is interactive; self-efficacy levels being determined via the interaction of perceived situational/task demands in terms of effort and difficulty, which are then matched against those perceptions which individuals make about their own abilities and capacity for effort. Self-efficacy has been shown to be significantly linked to performance and to the degree of persistence shown in the light of setbacks in task completion, with higher self-efficacy being related to improved performance and persistence. Training has also been shown to influence levels of self-efficacy as well as the type of training employed. The uniqueness of the approach is understood by appreciating that self-efficacy measures are centred on task and situation, that is, what people do rather than on competences which have been criticised for their lack of attention to the context in which they are deployed. Because of this task-centred approach, many of the problems of defining and assessing competences are overcome and questionnaires can be made role specific (Mark, 1993; Lane, 1992).

References

Abel-Smith, B. (1992) 'The reform of the National Health Service' *Quality Assurance in Health Care*, Vol. 4, No. 4, pp. 163–272.

Amidon, S. (1994) 'Overlong, overdue and over here', *The Sunday Times*, 8 May, Section 10, pp. 12–14.

Audit Commission (1995) *The Doctor's Tale* (London: HMSO).

Best, G. (1993) 'Keeping the doctors below deck', *Health Service Journal*, Vol. 103, No. 5357, p. 24, 17th June.

BMA (1995) *Core Values for the Medical Profession in the 21st Century* (London: BMA)

Burgogyne, J. and Lorbiecki, A. (1993) 'Clinicians into Management: the experience in context', *Health Services Management Research*, Vol. 6, No. 4, pp. 248–259.

Calman Report (1993) 'Hospital Doctors: training for the future: the report of a working group on specialist medical training' (London: Department of Health).

Charlwood, P. (1994) 'From ladders to climbing frames' MESOL Update 5, Spring 1994, p. 1 (NHSTD Bristol, Pub. No. 2560194).

DHSS (1974) *Management Arrangements for the Reorganised National Health Service* (London: HMSO).

DHSS (1986) *Resource Management (Management Budgeting) in Health Authorities*, HN(86)34 (London: DHSS).

DHSS (1989) *Working for Patients: the health service caring for the 1990s*, Cm. 55 (London: HMSO).

DoH (1992) *Funding of Hospital Medical and Dental Training Grade Posts* (London: NHMSE).

DoH (1993) *Managing the New NHS: proposals to determine new NHS Regions and establish new RHASs*, consultative document (Leeds: DoH).

DoH (1994) *The Challenges for Nursing and Midwifery in the 21st Century* (London: DoH).

DoH/NHSME (1993) *Final Report of the Middlesex University Evaluation of the Management Development Scheme for Hospital Consultants* (Leeds: NHSME Personnel Development Division).

Dopson, S. (1993) 'Management – the one disease consultants did not think existed', Management Research Paper, 94/2, pp. 1–13 (Oxford: Templeton College).

Edmonstone, J. and Havergal, M. (1995) 'The death (and rebirth?) of organisation development', *Health Manpower Management*, Vol. 21, No. 1, pp. 28–33.

Fitzgerald, L. and Sturt, J. (1992) 'Clinicians into management: on the change agenda or not?', *Health Services Management Research*, Vol. 5, No. 2, pp. 137–46.

French, J. and Raven, B. (1958) 'The bases of social power', in D. Cartwright (ed.) *Studies in Social Power* (Ann Arbor, Michigan: Institute for Social research).

Gibbs, I., McLaughan, D. and Griffiths, M. (1991) 'Skill Mix in Nursing: a selective review of the literature', *Journal of Advanced Nursing*, Vol. 16, pp. 242–9.

Glaser, R. and Chi, M.T.H. (1988) 'Overview' in Micheline, T.H., Chi, R.G. and Marshall, J. (eds) *The Nature of expertise* (Hillsdale NJ: Lawrence Erlbaum).

Gretton, I. (1994) 'It's time to help teachers manage', *Professional Manager*, Vol. 13, No. 6, pp. 18–19, November.

Ham, C. and Hunter, D.J. (1988) *Managing Clinical Activity in the NHS*. Briefing Paper No. 8 (London: King's Fund Institute).

Hancock, C. (1993) 'Whither nursing in the 1990s?' *Journal of Management in Medicine*, Vol. 7, No. 5, pp. 11–16.

Handy, C. (1984) 'Education for management outside business' in Goodlad, S. (ed.) *Education for the Professions*. Papers presented to the 20th Annual Conference of the Society for Research in Higher Education (Nelson: SRHE and NFER)

Harrison, S. and Pollitt, C. (1994) *Controlling Health Professionals – the future of work & organisation in the NHS* (Buckingham: Open University Press).

Harrison, S., Hunter, D.J., Marnoch, G. and Pollitt, C. (1993) *Just Managing: Power and Culture in the National Health Service* (Basingstoke: Macmillan).

HAS (1992) *Clinicians in Management* (Sutton: NHS Health Advisory Service).

Hoffenberg, R. (1986) *Clinical Freedom*, Rock Carling Fellowship Lecture (London: Nuffield Provincial Hospital Trust).

Holloway, W. (1991) *Work Psychology and Organisational Behaviour* (London: Sage).

Hopkins, A. (ed.) (1993) *The Synchromesh Report – the Role of Hospital Consultants in Clinical Directorates* (London: Royal College of Physicians/ Kings Fund).

HSJ (1992) 'Quotes of the Year', Dr Tony Hicklin, East Surrey delegate to the BMA's conference on NHS Reforms in 1992. *Health Services Journal* Vol. 102, No. 5333, p. 19, 17th December.

Huczynski, A. and Buchanan, D. (1991) *Organisational Behaviour: an Introductory Text* (Hemel Hempstead: Prentice Hall International).

Hunter, D. and Williamson, P. (eds) (1989) 'Perspectives on general management in the NHS', *Health Services Management Research*, Vol. 2, No. 1, pp. 2–9.

Iglehart, John K. (1994) 'Health Policy Report: Health Care Reform: the role of physicians', *New England Journal of Medicine*, Vol. 330, No. 10, pp. 728–31.

IHSM Consultants (1994) 'Creative Career Paths in the NHS, Report No. 1: Top Managers' (London: NHS Executive).

IHSM (1994) 'Appreciating the Value of Management', IHSM NOW Issue 54, June, pp. 1–2.

IHSM (1994a) 'Doctors in management: a symposium headed by the NHSME 11/1/94', *Management Development Quarterly*, No. 6, March, p. 5.

Jefferys, M. (1991) 'Sociological Health Policy Research for the 1990s' in *The Sociology of the Health Service* J. Gabe, M. Calnan and M. Bury (eds) (London: Routledge).

Kirkpatrick, D. (1960) 'Techniques for evaluating training programmes', *Journal of the American Society for Training and Development*', Vol. 14, No. 13–18, pp. 25–32.

Kolb, D.M. (1992) 'Women's work: peacemaking in organisations', in D.M. Kolb and J.M. Bartunek (eds) *Hidden Conflict in Organisations – uncovering behind-the-scenes disputes* (Newburg Park, Calif.: Sage).

Lane, J. (1992) 'Methods of Assessment', *Health Manpower Management*, Vol. 18, No. 2.

Lorbiecki, A., Snell, R. and Burgogyne, J. (1992) 'Final Report of the National Evaluation of the First Wave Management Development Initiative for Hospital Consultants' Lancaster University, pp. 1–39.

Lukes, S. (1974) *Power: a radical view* (London: Macmillan).

Lukes, S. (1986) 'Introduction' in S. Lukes (ed.) *Power* (Oxford: Blackwell).

Mackenzie, W.J.M. (1979) *Power and responsibility in Health Care: The national health service as a political institution* (Oxford: Oxford University Press).

MacLachlan, R. (1992) 'Clinically Unhinged', *Health Service Journal*, 1 October, p. 16.

Mark, A. (1991) 'Where are the medical managers?' *Journal of Management in Medicine*, Vol. 5, No. 4, p. 6–12.

Mark, A. (1991a) 'Clinical Directorates – Will the glass ceiling be double glazed?', *Health Manpower Management*, Vol. 17, No. 4.

Mark, A. (1993) 'Researching the Doctor Manager – choosing valid methodologies', *Journal of Management in Medicine*, Vol. 7, No. 4, pp. 52–9.

Mark, A. (1993a) 'Doctors into Managers – the personal costs'. Paper presented at conference on 'The personal costs of managerial work', Bolton Business School, 28–30 November.

Mark, A. (1994) *Supplementary Report of the Middlesex University Evaluation of the Management Development Scheme for Hospital Consultants in the Special Health Authorities* (Leeds: NHSME Personnel Development Division).

Mark, A (1994a) 'Do special health authority doctors make special managers', *Journal of Management in Medicine*, Vol. 8, No. 6, pp. 58–63.

Mark, A. (1994b) 'Outsourcing Therapy Services', *Health Manpower Management*, Vol. 20, No. 2, pp. 37–40.

Mark, A. (1995) 'Powerful values in the National Health Service: do they still exist?'. Paper presented at Imperial College School of Management

26 June 1995, as part of Seminar 5 of Cardiff Business /ESRC Series, 'Power and Values in Public Sector Markets: the experience of professionals'.

Mark, A. and Scott, H. (1992) 'Management in the National Health Service', in 'Rediscovering Public Services Management' L. Willcocks and J. Harrow (eds) (London: McGraw-Hill).

Maxwell, R. (1993) Chapter 9 in Hopkins, A. (ed.) *The synchromesh report – the role of hospital consultants in clinical directorates.* (London: Royal College of Physicians/King's Fund).

May, A. (1993) 'Full Circle', *Health Service Journal*, 7 October, pp. 24–5.

McKegney, C.P. (1989) 'Medical Education: a neglectful and abusive family system', *Family Medicine,* Vol. 21, No. 6, pp. 452–7.

Ministry of Health (1967) *First Report of the Joint Working Party on the Organisation of Medical Work in Hospitals* (Cogwheel Report) (London: HMSO).

Mintzberg, H. (1988) 'Planning on the left side and managing on the right', in Katz, R. (ed.) *Managing Professionals in Innovative Organisations: a collection of readings* (Cambridge Mass.: Ballinger).

Mintzberg, H. (1994) 'The fall and rise of strategic planning', *Harvard Business Review*, January/February, pp. 107–14.

Mole, V. and Dawson, S. (1993) 'Pole to Pole – special report on clinical management', *Health Services Journal*, Vol. 103, pp. 33–4.

New England Journal of Medicine (1984) 'Special Report', Vol. 310, No. 22, 31 May.

Newman, K. and Cowling, A. (1993) 'Management Education for Clinical Directors: an evaluation', *Journal of Management in Medicine*, Vol. 7, No. 5, pp. 27–35.

NHSE (1994) *Managing the New NHS: Functions and responsibilities in the new NHS* (Leeds: Department of Health).

NHSTD (1991) *Invitation to Tender: evaluation of management development for consultants* (second year) (London: NHSME).

Pascale, R. (1990) *Managing on the Edge – how successful companies use conflict to stay ahead* (London: Penguin).

Pheysey, D.C. (1993) *Organisational Culture – types and transformations* (London: Routledge).

Quinn, J.B. (1992) *Intelligent Enterprise – a knowledge and service-based Paradigm for Industry* (New York: Free Press).

Ranade, W. (1994) *A Future for the NHS?* (Harlow: Longman).

Revans, R. (1980) *Action Learning: new techniques for managers* (London: Blond and Briggs).

Smith, P. (1992) 'Consultants in management training: learning and doing', *Journal of Management in Medicine*, Vol. 6, No. 2, pp. 11–26.

Spurgeon, P. (1993) 'Resource Management: a fundamental change in managing health services', in *The New Face of The NHS* P. Spurgeon (ed.) (Harlow: Longman).

Stewart, R. (1983) *Choices for Managers* (London: McGraw-Hill).

Sutherst, J. and Glascott, V. (1994) *The Doctor-Manager* (Edinburgh: Churchill Livingstone).

Thompson, D. (1993) 'Developing managers for the 1990s' in *The New Face of The NHS* P. Spurgeon (ed.) (Harlow: Longman).

Tietjen, C. (1991) 'Management Development in the NHS', *Personnel Management,* May, pp. 52–5 .

Tremblay, M. (1993) 'Of confidence and identity: the doctor in management', in *The New Face of the NHS,* ed. P. Spurgeon (Harlow: Longman).

Turner, Barry A. (1988) 'Connoisseurship in the study of organisational cultures', in Bryman, A. (ed.) *Doing Research in Organisations* (London: Routledge).

Turner, Bryan S. (1995) *Medical Power and Social Knowledge* (London: Sage).

White, A. (1993) *Management for Clinicians* (London: Edward Arnold).

7 Beyond Fund-Holding

Duncan Keeley

INTRODUCTION

General practioner fund-holding was an idea hatched in the early 1980s but introduced only at a late stage into the NHS reforms outlined in the 1989 white paper *Working for Patients*. Giving large general practices a budget for drugs, staff and certain hospital services was seen as having a number of advantages. It would provide an incentive to GPs to make economic use of these resources; it would empower GPs to improve hospital services by acting as informed purchasers on behalf of their patients; and it would provide a method of cash-limiting important elements of NHS expenditure by devolving to GPs the responsibility for rationing their use.

Many general practices have embraced this new role with enthusiasm. But others, including many dynamic, efficient and well organised practices, have decided on principle not to join the scheme.[1] As a member of one such practice I propose, in this chapter, to outline the disadvantages of fund-holding for patients, for practices, and for the public good. Some of these disadvantages are already apparent; others are likely consequences of the continuation and extension of fund-holding. I will go on to suggest ways in which many of the advantages of fund-holding might be retained without the unsustainable expense and inequity of the system as it currently exists.

Despite the recent introduction of 'community funholding' (in which practices take a fund for community health services only) and experimental total purchasing projects, the predominant version of fundholding remains the original one, now termed 'standard' fundholding. It is to standard fundholding which the argument in this paper relates. In 1994–5 fundholders budgets accounted for roughly 9 per cent of all NHS expenditure. As of April 1996 just under 50 per cent of the population of England is registered with practices engaged in standard fundholding.

DISADVANTAGES OF FUND-HOLDING FOR PATIENTS

Patients go to doctors anxious to know whether their problem needs treatment, investigation, or referral to a specialist. They need to be confident that the doctor's recommendation is based purely on what they need and is not likely to be influenced by financial considerations. Patients of fund-holding GPs may be concerned, legitimately or otherwise, that their doctor's loyalty is divided between the role of advocate and the role of rationer of resources. There is a real risk that in future financial pressure on fund-holders may lead to patients being inappropriately denied access to the benefits of specialist medicine.

Patients suffer if the resources available for their medical care are reduced as a result of increased adminstrative costs. At a national level fund-holding has made an important contribution to the near-doubling in the proportion of NHS expenditure devoted to administration since the reforms.

Patients suffer if the time and energy of their doctor is diverted from consultation into administration. They also suffer if continuity of care is further reduced by practices taking on part-time assistants to cover sessions which partners spend on administrative work. Fund-holding is making an important contribution to both of these problems.

Patients need to have a choice of general practice. If fund-holding continues, high management costs are likely to lead to amalgamation of practices in order to achieve economies of scale. In many communities such amalgamations would lead to a major reduction in the choice of primary care provider available to patients.

DISADVANTAGES OF FUNDHOLDING FOR GPs

Fund-holding is based on a fundamental misconception of the proper role of the general practitioner. The general practitioner's job is to provide 'personal, primary and continuing care to individuals and families'. By acting as a gatekeeper to expensive secondary services the GP plays a vital role in maintaining the hitherto unparalleled cost-effectiveness of the National Health Service. That role will be made far more difficult if we lose our patient's trust in the basis on which we make our decisions on treatment and referral. The general practioner must decide what the patient needs from the health care system, meet that need within the practice if possible and seek help from others if not. It is not the GPs job to decide which of these needs the NHS can afford to meet. Such decisions are political, and while GPs must play an important part in this decision-making in an advisory capacity they should not take on a prominent and visible role in deciding which of their own patients get what.

Fund-holding greatly increases the adminstrative workload of GPs. Despite generous management allowances, fund-holding GPs are nevertheless involved in considerable amounts of (currently unpaid) administrative work. Coming on top of the large increase in administrative work resulting from the new contract, this extra burden takes time and energy away from patient care. Paying fund-holding GPs for the time they put into administration would raise the management costs of the scheme still further.

Fund-holding GPs are implicitly accepting responsibility for the adequacy of the provision of elective surgical services for their patients. Early fund-holders, benefiting as they have from disproportionate levels of funding[2] and leverage over provider units, have often been able to improve the service for their patients in this respect. But as greater stringency is applied to the allocation and management of funds and as more attention is paid to equity in the provision of services, fund-holding GPs may come to regret taking on this role and seek to relinquish it.

Fund-holding poses a threat in the longer term to the independence and identity of pratices. Pressures for the amalgamation of practices discussed above may lead to primary care practices of such a size that their individual members lose any sense of ownership or control of the organisation in which they work. This may suit the agenda of some health service managers but is probably not in the interests of patients, or doctors, or nurses, or administrative staff.

DISADVANTAGES OF FUND-HOLDING FOR THE PUBLIC GOOD

Fund-holding weakens the district planning of health services. Planning is crucial if limited resources for health care are to be used to best effect. But planning of hospital and community health services is now bedevilled by the uncertainty that results from dependence on multiple unpredictable short term contracts. By duplicating the purchasing function and diluting the resources available for it fund-holding threatens to reduce the potential benefits of the purchaser–provider split – the one unquestionably good idea embodied in the 1990 reforms. One Oxfordshire fund-holding GP, describing the local successes of fund-holding, was quoted as finding that 'one unexpected outcome has been the almost total destruction of the district health authority.'[3] While reports of the demise of Oxfordshire Health Authority may have been premature, there is no question that the effectiveness of district purchasing has been compromised by fund-holding and the resources allocated to it. In Oxfordshire in 1994–5 the cost of fund-holding administration was approximately £1 million, used for purchasing 20 per cent of health care services for about 40 per cent of the population. This sum does not include the costs incurred by health authorities in support for fund-holding. In the same year the cost of the district health authority's purchasing division – responsible for the remaining 90 per cent of purchasing – was approximately £2.4 million.[4] The latter sum included the budget for the department of public health medicine, to which fundholders made no contribution. Thus, as a purchasing system, fund-holding was over four times as costly as the district health authority. The weakening of district health authorities is of particular concern in view of the fact that the districts remain responsible for the great majority of NHS purchasing. In future, if fund-holding continues to divide and weaken the purchasing function, hospitals may have greater power to determine the services they provide than was the case before the reforms.

Fund-holding makes a major contribution to the increased administrative costs of the new NHS. Fund-holding practices receive large management and computerisation allowances – at least £43 000 per annum per practice, equivalent to the pay of one GP, or more than three nurses. General practice premises have had to expand their office space to house the new managers and their computers – a major use of fund savings. The complex contracting procedures with fund-holding practices in turn increase the cost and complexity of administrative functions in provider units. It is by no means clear that these costs are paid for by fund-holding practices and may constitute a further subsidy to fund-holding from district purchasers.

Fund-holding is leading to unplanned random transfer of resources from hospitals to the primary care sector. In the long term a switch of resources into primary care may be desirable, but under current conditions fund-holders' savings on their hospital budgets amount to a form of revenue stripping of an under-funded hospital service and work to the detriment of the provision of core services – and of elective surgery for the patients of non-fundholding practices. No satisfactory mechanism is in place for ensuring that fund-holders' savings – sometimes running to £100 00–£200 000 per annum – are used in a planned way to benefit patient care. Fundholders savings nationally – representing underspending on allocated budgets – amounted to £111 million by 1993–4, at which time only 17 per cent had actually been spent. Many of the practices making such savings are already very well resourced. In Oxfordshire in 1993 nearly 70 per cent of total fund savings were spent on building or extending GP's surgeries – in some cases for buildings owned by the practices concerned. Large savings were made on budgets for hospital services despite the fact, documented in Coulter's study of referrals in Oxford region[9] that referral rates to hospital from fundholding practices continued to increase. No evidence has been published from anywhere in the country to suggest that fundholding practices have reduced their use of hospital services. This must call into question the appropriateness of continued savings being made on the hospital services element of the fund. The opportunity to vire funds intended for hospital and community health services and medicines into the purchase of assets owned by general practitioners themselves constitutes an improper incentive to economise on these elements of the fund. It should cease.

Fund-holding risks diverting NHS resources into the private health care sector, to the detriment of NHS hospitals. A cynical observer might be tempted to the view that the hospital services chosen for inclusion within fund-holding were precisely those services which the private sector could compete to provide on favourable if unfair terms. The private sector largely confines its activities to profitable low risk elective procedures. It does not concern itself with expensive things like running casualty departments or intensive care units, or caring for the chronically sick (who can't get insurance), or training staff. Fundholders are showing gradually increasing readiness to use private sector services. Readers will differ in their views on whether or not the benefits resulting from the competition thus engendered outweigh the risks to the standard and comprehensiveness of public health care provision posed by diversion of NHS resources into the private sector.

Fund-holding has led to a two-tier service in the provision of elective surgery. There is overwhelming anecdotal evidence to the effect that the patients of fund-holding GPs have more rapid access to elective surgery on the NHS.[5] The lack of systematic evidence is a testament to the extraordinary failure of the NHS Management Executive to monitor the consequences of the reforms in this respect, and to a more general disinclination on the part of NHS management to do anything whatever which might call the wisdom of any aspect of the reforms into question. The post-Griffiths management culture in the health service renders this failure understandable but nonetheless saddening. The Executive should require all provider units to publish average waiting times from referral to surgery for a selection of surgical procedures by source of contract. It should require corrective action to be taken by district health authorities where evidence arises of systematically better access to elective surgery for the patients of fund-holding practices. Such action is necessary to restore public confidence in the continued fairness of the post-reform NHS. Ministers continue to insist that there should be no inequality of access to NHS services for the patients of fund-holding and non-fundholding practices. It should be for Ministers – not for journalists or GPs – to provide the evidence that this is indeed the case.

ARE FUND-HOLDERS MORE EFFECTIVE AS PURCHASERS?

Insofar as fund-holders have secured better hospital services for their patients, this has been attributed by some to their greater effectiveness as purchasers, as compared with district health authorities. In deciding the future shape of purchasing arrangements it is important to decide if this is the case, and if so, why.

Fund-holders have achieved some notable successes in pressing for better services from hospitals. In some cases the changes achieved have been to the benefit of all practices and patients in the locality. Their small size in comparison to district health authorities has allowed greater flexibility, and improvements in service have been achieved by the reality or the threat of relatively small shifts in resources. Fund-holders have been able to teach districts some important lessons in the art of stimulating change in patterns of hospital provision.

However, the greater effectiveness of fund-holders as purchasers needs to be seen in the light of the following considerations.

Firstly, some fund-holding practices have received disproportionately large budgets with which to purchase services. A recent analysis of budget allocations in North West Thames Region suggests that per capita allocations to fund-holding practices for hospital services were in some cases more than twice as high as the amounts effectively available to district health authority patients.[6] Such errors will be less likely in future. But progress towards a systematic capitation basis for calculating funds remains very slow, and may not prove feasible for such small populations.

Secondly, as argued above, fund-holders have been much more generously funded than district health authorities for the purchasing function itself. This could be corrected, either by greatly increasing the funding of the district purchasing departments (unlikely) or by reducing fund-holding management allowances (likely to lead to wholesale abandonment of fund-holding).

Thirdly, and uncorrectably, fund-holders have an unfair advantage by virtue of the fact that the budget for elective hospital services for their patients is ring-fenced, protected from the perennial excess demand for core and emergency services to which their patients continue to have equal access. The district health authority, responsible for providing the costly core and emergency services for the whole population, cannot accord equivalent priority to elective services – and the consequences of any shortfall are borne by the patients of non-fund-holding practices. This is unacceptable. Short of the phasing out of fund-holding, the only solution to this problem would be to ring-fence the budget for elective surgery at a national level: this would be likely to cause impossible pressures on core service provision in the absence of significant additional funding.

A BETTER SYSTEM FOR GP INVOLVEMENT IN PURCHASING: THE COMMISSIONING GROUP

As well as being very expensive, fund-holding is inadequate as a system for GP involvement in purchasing: firstly because it only covers a minority of the population and secondly because it only covers a minority of what the health service exists to provide. With limited resources it is a mistake to establish a separate purchasing system for elective as opposed to core services.

What is needed is a comprehensive system for advice to purchasers from primary care, a system of Commissioning Groups – based either at locality or district level. Such a system could be put in place in a short time and at a fraction of the current cost of fund-holding administration.

District health authorities could establish a network of locality outposts, each based in a locality serving 50–100 000 people. The locality office should be staffed by a full-time administrator and should retain on a sessional basis the services of general practitioners and community nurses. These sessional posts should carry good remuneration and a responsibility to collect and represent the views of local primary care teams and local populations to the district purchasing team, in whose decisions their views should carry appropriate weight. The posts should be made attractive to knowledgeable and respected local practitioners by good resourcing and support. Post-holders should have the opportunity of training in epidemiology and in the assessment of the evidence base for purchasing decisions. The posts should be subject to re-election/re-appointment on a three yearly basis. As experience grows in the management of purchasing at locality level the possibility exists of districts devolving part or all of their budgets for hospital and community services to the localities.

District health authorities will need to call on the experience, skills and tactics of GPs with experience of fund-holding. In particular they will need to appreciate the importance of being able to shift, or threaten to shift, small chunks of resource so as to be able to stimulate change in providers without jeopardising them.

Such a system of locality offices could be put in place for a cost of between £250 000 to £500 000 per district per annum. Such sums are beyond the reach of district health authorities' current resources for purchasing, but are considerably less than the amounts already being spent on the management costs of fund-holding. Further economies would result from the simplification of the contracting process within provider units. Much has already been achieved by non-fundholding consortia of GPs in some areas,[7] and these achievements have been managed on a shoestring. Nottingham Non-fundholders, providing purchasing advice for an entire health district, had a budget from the district health authority of £55 000 in 1994–5.[8] This is a sum only just in excess of the administrative funding available annually for a single fund-holding practice. In most districts the financial support for GP input into purchasing outwith fund-holding has been even less.

An alternative to the locality model outlined above is a single Commissioning Group at district level. This would probably cost less, but would lose the potential of the locality model for responsiveness to local needs and would achieve less widespread involvement of GPs and community nurses in the purchasing process. It would, however, be less vulnerable to differing levels of enthusiasm for and commitment to commissioning in different localities.

The size of population served by each GP Commissioning Group would no doubt vary in different parts of the country. But two key features distinguish Commissioning Groups from any fundholding model. Firstly, financial accountability, in commissioning, remains with the health authority and not with the doctors themselves. Secondly, commissioning involves general practitioners in a partnership with other players to achieve the best use of health service resources, rather than seeking to dictate and control how the money should be spent. For the great majority of GPs commissioning will be seen as the better way forward.

WHAT ABOUT COST CONTAINMENT?

From the Treasury perspective, a major attraction of fund-holding lay in its potential for containing the rise in health care costs. The study of prescribing costs by Bradlow and Coulter in Oxfordshire initially showed a lower rate of rise in these costs in fund-holding practices compared with non-fundholding controls.[9] The results of this study should be interpreted bearing in mind that the majority of the non-fundholding practices included in the control group are now either in or preparing for fund-holding. They may therefore have had an incentive to increase their prescribing costs so as to boost the eventual size of their prescribing fund. A follow up study of the same group of practices three years after the introduction of fundholding found no evidence that fundholding was curbing the rise in prescribing costs.[10]

There is further evidence that the method of using historic prescribing and referral costs to determine fund allocations may have acted as an incentive to practices to increase their use of these resources prior to entering the scheme. In Coulter and Bradlow's study of referrals the non-fundholding practices increased their referral rate by 20 per cent in one year to match the referral rate of the fund-holding practices – which also rose.[11] One fund-holding practice, delighted with its large savings on prescribing, used the pages of the British Medical Journal to advise non-fundholding practices to delay any cost saving initiatives until after they had joined the scheme.[12]

It is highly debatable whether our understanding of how prescribing costs or referral rates relate to quality of care is sufficient to justify policies which give doctors incentives to reduce them, particularly when these policies have the potential to undermine patients' trust in their doctors' decisions. If we accept such an approach to cost containment as legitimate, it makes little sense to confine its operation to a minority of practices. The incentive which has partially contained the prescribing costs of fund-holding practices is that of the opportunity to vire 100 per cent of any savings made on the indicative prescribing amount to other forms of patient care. This incentive could easily be extended to non-fundholding practices. Savings made on drug budgets could be held on the practice's behalf by health authorities and spent in consultation with the health authorities, on other forms of patient care. Until such a system is instituted the prescribing costs of non-fund-holding practices will continue to surge ahead – especially if new fund-holders continue to receive historically based allocations for prescribing.

WHERE IS THE EVIDENCE?

Many of the arguments which I have advanced against the continuation of fund-holding are based on induction rather than evidence. One of the most extraordinary features of the fund-holding experiment has been the almost complete failure to institute any methodical assessment of its effects. The work of Coulter and Bradlow cited above is the only piece of work available which has compared fund-holding and non-fundholding practices. Professor Howie's studies in Scotland[13,14] looks in detail at the process of medical care and at patient satisfaction, but use a group of practices taking up fund-holding as their own controls. Some commentators have felt able to pass highly favourable comment on the effects of fund-holding on the basis of uncontrolled observational studies of scant scientific merit.[15] Review articles[16,17] have suggested that few reliable conclusions, positive or negative, can be drawn from existing research. This dearth of objective data faces us with the need to make policy decisions on the basis of common sense – with all the strengths and weaknesses which that entails.

CONCLUDING REMARKS

Fund-holding is fatally flawed by the restrictions which were necessary to make it work at all. Restricted to a minority of practices it offends one of the fundamental principles of the National Health Service, the principle of equity. Restricted to a minority of procedures and services it introduces an illogical and unsatisfactory division between the purchasing of elective and core services. It is based on a misconception of the proper role of the general practitioner. If allowed to continue it will undermine patients' trust in doctors' decisions and will make it more difficult for doctors to provide the personal primary continuing care which is what their patients most want from them.

Fund-holding needs to be replaced by a less expensive but more comprehensive system of Commissioning Groups for primary care input into purchasing decisions. Like all quixotic adventures it will have taught us some useful things – but it can't last.

Notes

1. Keeley, D. (1993) 'The fundholding debate: should practices reconsider the decision not to fundhold?', *British Medical Journal* 306: 697–8.
2. Dixon, J., M. Dinwoodie, D. Hodson, *et al.* (1994) 'Distribution of NHS funds between fundholding and non-fundholding practices', *British Medical Journal*, 309: 30–4.
3. 'Quality forum pays off', *Fundholding* magazine, 7 October 1993. Interview with Dr Richard Stephenson.
4. *Finance and Activity Plan 1994–5.* Paper 35/94 Oxfordshire Health Authority.
5. *Fundholding and Access to Hospital Care.* Association of Community Health Councils. London, March 1994.
6. Dixon, J., et al. (1994) 'Distribution of NHS funds between fundholding and non-fundholding practices', *British Medical Journal*, 309: 30–4.

7. Shapiro, J. (1994) *Shared purchasing and collaborative commissioning within the NHS.* National Association of Health Authorities and Trusts. Birmingham. ISBN 1 85947 019 X.
8. Dr Alan Birchall, Chilwell Notts. Personal communication.
9. Bradlow, J. and A. Coulter (1993) 'Effect of fundholding and indicative prescribing schemes on general practitioners' prescribing costs', *British Medical Journal* 307: 1186–9.
10. Stewart-Brown, S., R. Surender, J. Bradlow, A. Coulter, H. Doll (1991) 'The effects of fundholding in general practice on prescribing habits three years after the introduction of the scheme', *British Medical Journal*, 311: 1543–7.
11. Coulter, A. and J. Bradlow (1993) 'Effect of NHS reforms on general practitioners' referral patterns', *British Medical Journal* 306: 433–7.
12. Dowell, J.S., D. Snadden, J.A. Dunbar (1995) 'Changes to generic formulary how one fundholding practice reduced prescribing costs', *British Medical Journal*, 310: 505–8.
13. Howie, J., D. Heaney, M. Maxwell *et al.* (1992) 'The Scottish General Practice Shadow Fund-Holding Project – Outline of an Evaluation'. *Health Bulletin* 50/4 July 316–28.
14. Howie, J., D. Heaney, and Maxwell, M. (1993) 'Evaluation of the Scottish Shadow Fund-Holding Project: First Results', *Health Bulletin* 51(2) March 94–105.
15. Glennerster, H., M. Matsaganis, P. Owens, and S. Hancock, (1994) 'G.P. Fundholding: Wild card or winning hand?' in Robinson R. and J. Le Grand J. (eds) *Evaluating the NHS Reforms* (Hermitage, Berks: Policy Journals).
16. Dixon, J. and H. Glennerster 'What do we know about fundholding in general practice?', *British Medical Journal* 311; 727–30.
17. Petchey, R. (1995) 'General practitioner fundholding: weighing the evidence', *Lancet*, 346: 1139–42.

8 Trust and Reputation in Community Care: theory and evidence

Russell Mannion and Peter Smith

INTRODUCTION

Central to the new quasi-markets in the public sector is the explicit articulation of relationships between purchasers and providers. Many authors have therefore noted the relevance of the economic literature relating to principals and agents to such markets. Indeed one of the side-effects of the quasi-market reforms has been a flourishing interest in models of public sector procurement. Much of the discussion relating to such models has noted the importance of *trust* in almost all such markets, notwithstanding the reliance on formal contracts to articulate responsibilities. This chapter therefore explores the part played by trust in one particular agency relationship: that between local government purchasers and providers of social care, set up in the UK Government's 'Community Care' reforms. However the results are likely to be applicable to many other quasi-markets.

In this context, community care comprises a variety of services designed to help those affected by problems associated with physical disability, learning difficulties, mental illness and old age. The intention is to enable such people to lead as independent a life as possible. The 'product' that comprises community care is immensely complex, and there is an inevitable need for a great deal of trust between purchaser and provider. The chapter therefore begins with a general exposition of the relevant principal–agent model, and the role that trust may play in it. There is then a brief exposition of the community care reforms, and a discussion of the relevance of the principal–agent model. We describe an empirical study of observations relating to trust made by local authority officers involved in the new arrangements. Finally, we discuss the findings in the light of the theoretical literature.

The overwhelming evidence from our study is that providers in the community care market compete mainly on the basis of trust and reputation, rather than on price. Because of the problems of defining, measuring and monitoring the quality of care, purchasers have to rely on information relating to reputation and trust when assessing the performance of providers. In this market, purchasers are highly risk averse, and appear to treat price as a constraint. They then search for what they perceive to be the best quality provider, subject to that constraint. These findings have important implications for the functioning of the market in community care.

PRINCIPALS, AGENTS AND TRUST

Many models of principals and agents have been reported. However, the components of such models which are germane to this paper are as follows:

a) there is a principal who wishes to delegate some task to another party;
b) there is at least one agent who is willing to undertake such a task;
c) there exists a difference in the utility functions of the two parties;
d) there is a legally binding contract between the two parties which cannot specify all the characteristics of the task desired by the principal (it is incomplete);
e) there is some sort of information imperfection, usually in the form of an asymmetry between principal and agent.

The contract entails some form of remuneration for the agent for completing the task according to the contract. The principal's utility is based on the quality with which the task is accomplished – some of which cannot be specified in the contract – and the remuneration paid to the agent. The agent's utility is assumed to be based on remuneration and the effort (or cost) expended. The information asymmetry may mean that the principal cannot know the actual costs or effort incurred by the agent. The situation may be further complicated by environmental uncertainty. Under these circumstances, agents may misrepresent their competence (adverse selection) or may mislead the principal about their level of effort (moral hazard).

Such agency relationships give rise to transaction costs borne by the principal because of the need to delegate the task. These costs may include the costs of searching for and validating agents, writing contracts, monitoring outcomes, and paying agents any necessary incentives. Williamson (1975) has developed the notion of transaction costs, and has argued that in some circumstances it may be optimal for a principal to 'internalise' transaction costs by setting up a bureaucracy rather than relying on a market. He notes that the situations in which a bureaucracy is likely to be optimal are those in which the market is not properly contestable: that is, when transaction costs occur frequently, when there is a high degree of uncertainty, or when there is high asset specificity. Conversely, a market is likely to be preferred when the market is contestable (which implies a low risk of opportunism, a high degree of certainty, and a low number of simple transactions).

However, as Arrow (1974) notes, another means whereby a principal can economise on transaction costs – even when a market is not properly contestable – is to use a trusted agent. He summarises the obvious advantages of trust as a control mechanism as follows. 'Trust is an important lubricant of a social system. It is extremely efficient; it saves people a lot of trouble to have a fair degree of reliance on other people's word' (Arrow, 1974, p. 23).

Trust is therefore often likely to be central to relationships between principal and agent, particularly in circumstances where outcomes are difficult to monitor, or where there is great environmental uncertainty. If an agent is trusted by the principal, it may be possible to economise on contracting costs and monitoring costs. If a principal is trusted by the agent, the agent's perception of risk may be reduced, and a lower contract cost ensue.

The transaction cost approach recognises that the propensity for opportunistic behaviour differs among contractors, and that it may be cost-effective for principals to commit resources to discriminating between potential agents. The models developed by Laffont and Tirole (1993) investigate the means whereby such discrimination may be effected. Within such models, trust can be thought of as a commodity which 'economises on the costs of bargaining, monitoring, insurance and dispute settlement' (Sako, 1991). This is because well-founded trust reduces behavioural uncertainty and increases the likelihood that promises will be honoured. To that end, Sako identifies three distinct kinds of trust, which address different aspects of the agency model:

contractual trust (based on the parties adhering to specific written or oral agreements); *competence* trust (which is concerned with the likelihood of the agent performing in a competent fashion); and *goodwill* trust (which is concerned with the willingness to go beyond the mere fulfilment of explicit promises to taking initiatives to assist the other party, and to resist taking advantage of incomplete contracts).

Thus neo-classical economics has recognised the relevance of trust to the agency problem. However, it has so far developed few analytical tools with which to investigate the role that trust plays in economic transactions. It is therefore instructive to move outside the neo-classical economics tradition to explore the notion of trust from a behavioural and sociological perspective. In this context, it is worth recalling that the market has not always been the analytical preserve of economic theory. For instance in *The Wealth of Nations* (1776), Adam Smith drew no sharp distinction between economic and sociological themes. This integrative tradition continued into the nineteenth century, until economists became convinced that the discipline could progress only if a series of simplifying assumptions were made that entailed formalising their analysis with the aid of mathematics. Subsequent interpretation of the market has been dominated by ahistorical and asocial analysis, in particular in the form of neo-classical and Austrian economics (for a fuller discussion see Lunt, Mannion and Smith, 1996).

Recent years have witnessed renewed interest in integrating social and economic theories of human behaviour. In the 1960s economists such as Gary Becker extended neo-classical models to areas such as marriage and immigration, traditionally the preserve of sociologists. Many social scientists viewed this 'rational choice sociology' as a form of economic imperialism and it was not until the early 1980s that sociologists, particularly those based at Harvard University such as Mark Granovetter and Harrison White, revived interest in applying sociological theory to the study of market processes. Although economic sociology draws on many different sources, three central assumptions can be identified (Granovetter and Swedberg, 1982).

a) the pursuit of economic goals is normally accompanied by pursuit of non-economic goals such as sociability, approval, status and power;
b) economic action (like all action) is socially situated, and cannot be explained by individual motives alone; it is embedded in ongoing networks of social relations rather than carried out by atomised actors;

c) economic institutions (like all institutions) do not arise automatically in some form made inevitable by external circumstances, but are socially constructed.

Clearly it may well be the case that the New Economic Sociology can be used to shed light on how relationships of trust are developed and maintained between purchasers and providers in community care.

In recognising the importance of trust, it is important to develop a clear idea of what is meant by the concept. The Oxford English Dictionary defines trust as 'faith or confidence in the loyalty, strength, veracity, etc.; of a person or thing', and defines the economic usage of the term as 'confidence in the ability and intention of a buyer to pay at a future time for goods supplied without present payment'. However, such definitions are of limited usefulness for our purposes. Instead, we take as a starting point the definition of the concept of trust developed by Gambetta (1988) for use in the social sciences:

> trust (or, symmetrically, distrust) is a particular level of subjective probability with which an agent assesses that another agent or group of agents will perform a particular action, both before he can monitor such action (or independently of his capacity ever to be able to monitor it) and in a context in which it affects his own action. (Gambetta, 1988, p. 217).

A number of interesting points arise from this definition. First, trust can be viewed as a point on a probability distribution which can take any value from complete distrust (0) to complete trust (1). For example, a principal's level of trust in an agent is likely to have been formed in the light of the agent's previous behaviour, which gives rise to a reputation. In this context blind trust (loyalty) or blind distrust represents lexicographic predispositions to maintain the extreme values even when experience does not support this.

Second, the concept of trust is especially applicable to situations of ignorance or uncertainty about unknown or unknowable actions of others. Therefore trust does not relate generally to all an agent's future actions, but only to those future actions which affect present decisions. Therefore the existence of ignorance or uncertainty is fundamental to the importance of trust. In the context of the principal–agent model, trust has particular relevance to a) the information asymmetry between principal and agent and b) the response of the agent to environmental uncertainty. Trust would not assume such importance if the principal could observe the agent's effort levels, could foresee all possible future contingencies and design enforceable contracts to accommodate them.

Third, the concept of trust is based on the expectation that an agent has sufficient freedom and predisposition to disappoint the principal's expectations. If agents were heavily constrained by the form of their contracts, or had utility functions which were similar to those of their principals, there would be less concern on the part of principals about the likelihood of agents performing in accordance with their wishes. Indeed trust has been defined as a device for coping with the freedom of others (Luhmann, 1979; Dunn, 1988). Similarly, for trust to be of relevance, a principal must possess the freedom to choose whether or not to enter into a risky relationship with a particular agent. If the principal has no alternative agent, then the relationship is one of dependency and hope rather than trust.

Arising from this discussion, the concept of *reputation* for trustworthiness can be viewed as a capital asset. Although a reputation for trustworthiness is usually acquired gradually, it can be destroyed very quickly. Dasgupta (1988) contends that reputation should be considered using the language of probabilities. An agent's reputation is the principal's inference of the agent's position along the probability distribution noted above. Thus a potential agent is likely to be eager to establish a good reputation, and to that end it may be optimal for an agent to put resources into enhancing its reputation for trustworthiness. Agents may seek to do this through their actions (demonstrating a history of good performance) or through their marketing effort.

THE NEW COMMUNITY CARE

Before the introduction of community care in 1993, social care services had been provided and funded by a range of agencies, including the National Health Service, local government and the Benefits Agency. The new arrangements gave local authorities the lead responsibility for assessing the requirements of and arranging a suitable package of services for those in need of social care. The Government set out a number of objectives for community care, which included allowing people to continue to live as independently as possible in their own homes, the promotion of the independent sector of social care provision, and securing better value for taxpayers' money. Central to the new arrangements is the establishment of a market in social care, in which the local authority purchases services on behalf of its clients, and a range of providers compete to deliver the required services. A 'quasi-market' in community care has therefore been established, along the lines of those already operating in health and education in the UK (Le Grand and Bartlett, 1993; Bartlett *et al.*, 1994). The principal feature of community care which distinguishes it from these other publicly funded quasi-markets is that it is an *external* market, in which many providers are drawn from the independent sector, and that many of the providers are likely to be profit-seeking.

The duties placed on local authorities in relation to community care are set out in the 1990 National Health Service and Community Care Act. The practice guidance issued by the Social Services Inspectorate (SSI) sets out the general framework within which local authorities are to purchase social care services (Department of Health, 1991). The document recommends that social service departments obtain the necessary information in order to asses whether potential suppliers are reliable, commercially viable and share the values of the purchasing authority (Hudson, 1994). Part II of the Local Government Act 1988 prevents local authorities from specifying non-commercial considerations in contracts (for example, terms and conditions of employment, staff promotion and training) although matters such as staff qualifications, ability to recruit and retain staff as well as likely ability to meet the terms of the contract, can be taken into account when selecting providers.

As with most procurement in the state sector, the principal mechanism for allocating resources and controlling activity is the contract between purchaser and provider. The SSI guidance identifies three ways in which local authorities can select providers: open tendering, in which all providers are invited to tender; select list tendering, in which providers are short-listed on certain criteria, thereafter competing mainly on price; and direct negotiation with suppliers, whereby service specifications are developed jointly between purchasers and providers.

In discussing the purchase of community care it is important to bear in mind the important distinguishing features of the services being bought. First, the requirements of individual users are likely to be diverse. A key objective of the reforms was to match services more closely to needs, and for this to be achieved it is not possible to rely on standard packages of care. Second, the needs of users are likely to be unpredictable, and to change over time. The system of care must therefore be flexible and responsive. Third, at the same time, continuity of care is vitally important, with changes in provider potentially very damaging to the individual. Fourth, many users are vulnerable individuals who need to be protected from exploitation. And fifth, there is an intrinsic difficulty in specifying and monitoring quality standards in community care, particularly relating to eventual outcomes. In many ways the quasi-market in community care is therefore about as complex a market as can be envisaged. The product is multi-dimensional and evolves over a period of time. It is impossible to specify complete contracts. And an intermediary is purchasing on behalf of the beneficiary.

THIS STUDY

We undertook fieldwork in six social service departments, chosen to reflect a wide range of circumstances.[1] The year studied was 1994/5, the second year of implementation. About five managers in each department were interviewed using qualitative, semi-structured interviews. The interviewees were chosen so as to elicit perceptions at all levels in the managerial hierarchy at which some element of discretion regarding resource allocation existed. In all areas, this included the Assistant Director of Social Services responsible for community care at the top of the hierarchy. The lowest level in most local authorities was team manager, directly responsible for care managers, the front line staff who arrange assessments and manage care packages.[2] The interviews covered the following issues: organisational structure; budgeting and financial control; the local market in providers; transaction costs; and the process of provider choice. In this chapter we focus on the issues relating to trust that were raised by the respondents.

This work adds a growing body of research into the community care quasi-market. Before implementation of the reforms a number of commentators speculated on the likely impact of the introduction of market principles to community care (Hudson, 1992; Hoyes and Means, 1993).

The School for Advanced Urban Studies at the University of Bristol embarked on a programme of research in Community Care (Bartlett *et al.*,1994). The Nuffield Institute for Health (University of Leeds) and the Personal Social Services Research Unit (University of Kent at Canterbury), on behalf of the Department of Health, have jointly researched the implementation of the community care reforms in 25 social services authorities in England. This follows a similar survey conducted in the same representative sample of authorities in 1991. Data collection for this survey was largely based on interviews with directors and chairs of social services (Wistow *et al.*, 1994). The Audit Commission is also monitoring the implementation of community care, particularly the financial implications of the new system (Audit Commission, 1993; 1994). A number of academics have also applied economic theory to the community care market (Lunt, Mannion and Smith, 1996; Lapsley and Llewellyn, 1994; Smith and Wright, 1994; Forder, 1995).

FINDINGS

In most of the local authorities involved in the study, community care budgets were devolved down to team leader level. However we found that front line care managers were generally given a high degree of discretion over the actual choice of provider for a given user, although expenditure on services may first have to be agreed with a line manager – usually the team leader. In the first instance a package of care for a new applicant is designed on the basis of a formal assessment of his or her care needs. In this discussion we treat the recommended package of care as given, and concentrate on the role of trust in the choice of provider once that recommendation has been made. Our interviews revealed that, when a user expresses a preference for a particular provider, that preference is usually respected, provided the associated price is satisfactory. However many users and carers do not express a preference. Indeed for a variety of reasons it is often considered unreasonable or inappropriate to expect vulnerable people to take responsibility for individual purchasing decisions.[3] Our discussion therefore focuses on the choice of provider made by the local authority in the absence of an expressed user preference.

As we explain elsewhere, there are a plethora of macro factors that influence the choice of providers (Mannion and Smith, 1995). In this chapter we take these as given, and concentrate on the influences on choices for individual users. We illustrate the discussion with verbatim quotations from interviews with social services staff. Since our interview sample was small (30) and not intended to be statistically representative of the general population of social services staff, the findings outlined here cannot be generalised in a quantitative manner. Rather our analysis provides illustrations and explanations, and seeks to explore the social and behavioural dynamics underpinning market transactions.

Our interviews revealed that price and quality were the two crucial considerations in the choice of provider, although there was usually not an explicit trade off between the two. All of the authorities in the survey had broad guidelines outlining how much to spend on a particular type of service. Indeed in the residential sector there are nationally pre-scribed guidelines. Purchasers tend only to consider providers who fall within these guidelines and go outside them only in exceptional cir-cumstances. Typically, therefore, the choice of provider was the out-come of a sequential decision making process, in which – if price fell within acceptable and defined limits – quality was the crucial consider-ation in the choice of provider:

> We were [originally] going to have tendered prices and go for the cheapest option. But what we've actually done is develop a directory of providers who meet our general requirements. We don't necessar-ily go for the cheapest price. We have one provider in the [area] who is cheaper than the rest, but we only trust them with a few places be-cause they keep making a cock-up of it . . . I think we are learning more and more that you get what you pay for. (Assistant Director)

In practice, virtually all notions of quality in community care defy defi-nition. Consequently, purchasers have to rely on information relating to trust and reputation as the basis of assessing the quality of providers, given that they satisfy the price criterion. The perceived reputation for trustworthiness was particularly important in influencing the choice of domiciliary providers. Many of our interviewees explained that this was because it is very difficult to monitor the quality of services pro-vided in users own homes:

> Trust is important and increasingly so, particularly in the non-resi-dential sector as you don't have the back-up of the residential unit. It

is also much more difficult to monitor, although this is crucial. Chances are that there will be someone on duty every night, but with domiciliary services there is no back up and someone could die in the night. So you can't afford the risks. (Assistant Director)

Quality measures are not terribly applicable in a domiciliary setting where the workplace is someone's own home. We've had good organisations fail badly. One person working in a dispersed workforce cannot be monitored all the time. We don't have the staff to do the monitoring. This is the biggest grief. (Principal Manager)

We found that in many areas it was sometimes difficult or even impossible to obtain information regarding the trustworthiness of some potential providers. This was particularly so amongst domiciliary providers because many of them are new to the market and have yet to establish a reputation for trustworthy or untrustworthy behaviour:

We don't know enough about the providers out there. We've never dealt with the independent sector before – the Department of Social Security dealt with them. We don't know who is good, bad or indifferent. We need more information and monitoring to see if we trust some more than others. (Director of Finance)

Thus, in the early years of the new community care, many purchaser–provider relationships are characterised more by hope and dependency than by trust. As the market matures, a (positive) reputation for trustworthiness will offer providers an important competitive advantage. For this reason, it is always likely to be difficult for new entrants to establish themselves in the market in community care, and it is doubtful whether the market can ever be truly contestable.

Although the domiciliary sector was the preoccupation of many respondents, we found that a reputation for trustworthiness was also an important factor in the choice of residential home:

'The social workers seem to get to know particular homes by reputation and these they tend to favour . . . when they get good feedback from people or when the homes are obliging. We have some homes who do over and above what you would expect them to. Things like that social workers log in their minds and these are the homes they go to first. (Area Manager)

Given the importance of trust, the question therefore arises: how do purchasers form their views about the relative trustworthiness of competing providers? We encountered four possible ways in which information about the quality of providers could be transmitted to those with purchasing decisions: inspection; feedback from users; informal networks; and provider marketing.

Formal inspection is a statutory requirement for independent residential homes who wish to be registered as potential community care providers – they must be inspected twice a year. The system was generally felt to be inadequate, and there was perceived to be a lack of commitment to the formal inspection process:

> The registration system is inadequate. The nursing home where we had problems had one registration and inspection officer who covers 23 clinics and nursing homes. A mad and unsustainable situation. (Area Manager)

Moreover, formal inspection mechanisms may have a deleterious effect on the flow of information:

> One of the things that changed under the community care legislation was that the registration and inspection reports had to be made public. Prior to that they were not. This resulted in a huge change in the type of report [inspectors] put out. The original ones which were confidential had lots of subjective opinion, gut feeling, anecdotes etc. As soon as they became public and there was a risk of a challenge it suddenly changed dramatically. So although the information now appears to be more formal, I suspect that over telephones, over lunch, a lot of what was written down before is now transmitted verbally and is not put in a report. Informal networks are now used because they can't be challenged legally. Informal networks have always been the biggest source of communication in any local authority. (Director of Finance)

The domiciliary sector is not regulated in the same way, but most authorities have already implemented or are in the process of implementing an approved registration scheme.

User feedback was generally felt to be haphazard, partial, incomplete and difficult to record systematically. Some authorities had experimented with a limited range of user satisfaction surveys. However, the consensus was that this area merited much more vigorous development. In line with experience in the health care sector, there was some scepticism about the ability of user satisfaction surveys to capture the performance of providers (Carr-Hill, 1992), and some respondents suggested that the most desirable development in this area would be a responsive complaints procedure.

Informal networks amongst care managers were seen to be of vital importance:

> Information gets passed round by word of mouth. It's richer information but I'm not sure that it's comprehensive and consistent, and it doesn't address the problem with the [provider]. The word of mouth may be not to use agency x, but agency x will wonder why no one is using them any more – they will not be told necessarily why. (Team Leader)

However, once again there was considered to be a problem in moving from informal information towards a more formal recording of data:

> The information is informal. I've been trying to get it all put on a database so that we can swap it with other team leaders. (Team Leader)

Perhaps the most obvious link of trust exists between purchasers and their former colleagues in local authority providers. Indeed, the most formal evidence of trust is embodied in the existence of a large block contract with a particular provider, which is often formerly local authority run residential accommodation. The existence of such a contract will inevitably encourage the care manager to recommend use of that provider where appropriate.

Increasingly, the *marketing effort* by independent providers is being aimed at local authority purchasers:

> We get piles of stuff every week. I get a lot of phone calls. The most persistent ones will insist on coming here. We have no financial incentives to give business to specific agencies. I do know that [another area] were getting crates of beer and boxes of chocks, champagne, etc. (Team Leader)

The danger of improper influence of local authority workers was recognised:

> Now they are marketing it to us whereas before they were selling it to people out there . . . One of the things I wrote into the contracts from the start was the standard corruption clause. Any incentive or bribery will lead to the termination of a contract and possible prosecution. My limit to our staff who visit homes is to accept a cup of coffee, but lunch is questionable, an offer of a round of golf is definitely questionable. (Director of Finance)

In response to a lack of detailed knowledge about the quality of or the trustworthiness of specific providers, local authority purchasers often resorted to 'rules of thumb' about the probable trustworthiness of specific types of providers. Some authorities tended to favour voluntary sector providers because they were perceived to have more experience in providing social care services and are generally thought to put the interests of the user before financial gain:

> My experience is that in terms of trustworthiness, voluntary services have a better track record because they have more experience. They have a long history. Some of the private organisations have only been going a short space of time and haven't got the experience, the infrastructure and systems set up. Voluntary services have better quality control systems. (Assistant Director)

Alternatively some managers were more inclined to put their trust in private sector providers because they perceive that they have better management control systems and deliver more efficient services:

> I'd tend to opt for private providers as I trust them more. They are on more of a business footing and geared up to provide more cost-effective services. (Team Leader)

It is also evident that as the community care market becomes more established networks of trust and co-operation are increasingly developing between purchasers and providers. Purchasers welcomed this because it helps reduce the transaction costs associated with contract setting and dispute settlement:

We started off as the macho purchaser. But as there has been more contact between social workers, team leaders and providers, then the trust has been built up and it has reached the point where a provider can say 'You're daft paying all this money for all these services – why don't you do it in such and such a way?' You are now getting a culture of cooperation which helps promote certain standards and procedures. (Principal Manager)

The apparent lack of importance attached to price and the reliance on trust and reputation criteria should also be seen in the light of the utility function of the care managers. They are predominantly social workers, whose professional ethos reflects values such as 'respect, individualisation, confidentiality and self-determination' (Rojek, Peacock and Collins, 1988). The managerial ethic on which the reforms are based is therefore likely to be alien to the typical care manager. The utility of the care manager will also inevitably include private goals, such as job preservation and career advancement, which may be in conflict with the interests of users (Smith and Wright, 1994). Moreover, the service being purchased is usually complex, and purchasers are making what might be a long-term commitment, in which the costs of an unsatisfactory decision are potentially very high for the user, for carers and for the manager. In this respect information relating to reputation and trust is highly valued, as care managers are likely to be highly risk averse. As one area manager in the study explained:

A lot of information is based on reputation and past experiences of the services. From the workers' point of view they know if there's going to be any come-back, then it will be to them. So they have a lot at stake in the decision.

Therefore, for the risk-averse front-line manager, in the presence of hard cash limits, the incentive is to adopt strict criteria for accepting an applicant into community care. The available budget will then be spent on trustworthy providers for high need users – even though this may mean being able to accept fewer low need individuals into care. In this way, purchasing managers can minimise the damaging consequences to their clients and to themselves of placements with untrustworthy providers. Thus the pattern of care emerging under a strictly cash limited budget is likely to be – as one manager put it – 'a Rolls Royce for a few rather than a Metro for everyone'.

Our interviews with social services staff therefore revealed the importance that is attached to the reputation and trustworthiness of providers. Indeed the overwhelming evidence from this study suggests that community care providers compete largely on the basis of perceived reputation and trust rather than on price. Typically, price was treated as a constraint, with purchasers seeking to find the maximum quality provider subject to that constraint. Thus the choice of provider conforms to the sort of lexicographic model of consumer choice developed in the behavioural economics literature, in which a selection results from the satisfaction of a sequence of constraints, rather than from a simultaneous optimisation of all factors (Earl, 1983).

A number of factors contribute to the reliance on trust, most importantly the great difficulty experienced in defining, measuring and monitoring the quality of services, and the risk aversion of purchasers. These factors compel local authority purchasers to enter into trusting relationships with providers, and contracts tend to be awarded to those providers who establish a long term reputation for trustworthiness. The consequence of this for the behaviour of providers is that, in order to establish market share, there is a strong incentive for providers to commit resources to building up their reputation, using a variety of strategies. Reputation is a large intangible asset, and it is therefore unlikely that the community care market will ever be truly contestable.

DISCUSSION

Trust is a vital element in virtually all human transactions, and our study confirms that trust and reputation are of central importance in the operation of the new community care market. This is inevitable given the informational difficulties and uncertainties associated with community care, and the risk-aversion of purchasers. Without some reliance on trust the market would fail to operate. If purchasers trust providers, they can economise on the costs of writing and monitoring contracts. If providers trust purchasers, they will be prepared to make long term commitments, and to provide services which lie outside the strict terms of the contracts. New (1995) characterises such a relationship as a partnership.

Whenever trust is important, providers will seek to establish a reputation for trustworthiness. We have identified a number of marketing strategies they may adopt to this end. However, they may also seek to establish a reputation by their actions – by delivering high quality services. In order for this strategy to be perceived to be worthwhile, risk averse providers will need to know that their current actions will affect future outcomes, and that winning future contracts will to some extent depend on those outcomes. The dynamics of the community care market are therefore vital. It would seem that a reliance on trust as a lubricant of the market will go hand in hand with the development of long term relationships between purchasers and providers.

Furthermore, the concept of reputation as an important fixed asset suggests that there will be considerable barriers to entry in the community care market, and that there will be great pressure for purchasers to rely on long term relationships with a small number of trusted providers. This being the case, the market is unlikely to be contestable, and there will emerge considerable scope for oligopolistic exploitation on the part of providers. Therefore, for an efficient outcome to materialise, it is likely that purchasers will need to be constantly vigilant. They will need systematically to verify that the trust invested in a provider is based on good performance, rather than on skilful marketing strategies. It will be interesting to see what monitoring strategies emerge as the market matures.

More generally, the importance of trust should be reflected in the information systems developed to monitor the new community care. Bennett (1995) notes that the health internal market reforms may have *reduced* the amount of information available to purchasers, because of the disruption to informal sources of information they caused. This study of community care suggests that subjective issues and informal data are likely to be an important factor in many purchasing decisions. The designers of information systems should therefore seek to identify how any data that are collected can support such decisions. If they are not sensitive to the behavioural aspects of the decision-making process, it is possible that a great volume of unnecessary or inappropriate data will be collected.

Our findings on trust should be viewed within the context of the models of procurement set out by Laffont and Tirole (1993). They argue that, where quality is an important consideration, fixed price contracts may be appropriate only where the provider is sufficiently eager to preserve his or her reputation. In the absence of such eagerness, a cost-plus contract may be more appropriate. Thus the extent to which purchasers rely on reputation (as gained by actions) is likely also to affect the nature of the optimal contractual relationship. There is therefore a great deal of potential for exploring optimal incentive structures in this market (Forder, 1995).

We have noted that price does not appear to play a major part in the purchasing decision. This accords with sociological approaches to the market, in which a recurrent theme is the notion that traditional neo-classical economic theory overstates the role of price in regulating patterns of exchange (Bradach and Eccles, 1991). Purchasing decisions (at both an individual and organisational level) are assumed to be determined less by costs and demand, but rather are socially constructed through a process of bargaining within networks of social actors.

However, although we have emphasised the importance of the sociological view of market transactions, most of our discussion has been from a neo-classical principal–agent viewpoint. A fundamental component of the principal–agent model is the difference in the utility functions of principals and agents, a difference which is considered exogenous to the model. Yet enormous gains to both parties can be realised if those utility functions can be brought closer together. Our findings relating to trust suggest that principals in the community care market place a high value on finding agents whose objective functions are close to their own. This being the case, it is interesting to speculate on possible strategies that may *encourage* providers to adopt objectives which are close to those of the purchasers. One such, as noted above, is to nurture long term relationships. A further strategy on the part of purchasers – which is currently unfashionable – may be to encourage a sense of public service and professional duty amongst providers. This is the notion of 'clan control' advocated by Ouchi (1979) in situations of great uncertainty. In effect, the nature of the community care market may lead purchasers effectively to abjure the market, and to 'reinvent' the hierarchy.

In short, trust is always likely to be a central feature of the market in community care. The way in which purchasers treat trust will have implications for transaction costs, market structure and contractual form. Purchasers who ignore the importance of trust may incur excessive transaction costs (as they seek to control untrusted providers) and suffer low quality services (as providers fail to respond to user needs). On the other hand, an excessive reliance on trust leads to the possibility of opportunistic providers taking advantage of trusting purchasers in the form of poor quality and high prices. Our study therefore raises some fundamental question such as: what is the optimal extent to which trust should be used to economise on transaction costs in the community care market? how should a reliance on trust be made operational? and how can purchasers ensure that their trust is well founded?

In investigating these issues, our argument suggests that empirical analysis of the market is likely to benefit from methodological approaches which focus on the social context of market transactions. For example, Burt (1992) shows how it is possible to develop network models of relationships in competitive markets which are amenable to quantification. It is therefore quite likely that researchers will be able to develop testable hypotheses relating to trust in the community care market. However, the emphasis on relationships intrinsic to any analysis of trust suggests that relentless individualism of the neo-classical approach may in this respect be of limited usefulness.

Notes

1. The authorities include two London boroughs, two metropolitan districts and two non-metropolitan countries.
2. Anonymity of respondents was guaranteed, and so we are unable to give details of staff interviewed.
3. There is some support for a system of direct payments to users, who would therefore be free to purchase care without the mediation of the local authority. Such an arrangement would transfer the role of purchasing and monitoring care to the individual, and would limit the role of the local authority to that of needs assessor and financier. However, most respondents thought that there would be inherent problems with an indiscriminate direct payment scheme, given the vulnerability of many users. They felt that the most beneficial use of direct payments may be amongst younger disabled people.

References

Arrow, K. (1974) *The Limits of Organization* (New York: Norton).
Audit Commission (1993) *Taking Care: progress with community care* (London: HMSO).
Audit Commission (1994) *Taking Stock: progress with community care* (London: HMSO).

Bartlett, W., C. Propper, D. Wilson, and J. Le Grand (eds) (1994) *Quasi-Markets in the Welfare State* (Bristol: SAUS Publications).

Bennett, C. (1995) 'Health care and risk in the new NHS: issues around commissioning services', paper presented to ESRC conference *Risk in organizational settings*, (London, May).

Bradach, J.L. and R.G. Eccles (1991) 'Price, authority and trust: from ideal types to plural forms', in Thompson, G., J. Francis, R. Levačić and J. Mitchell, (eds) *Markets, Hierarchies and Networks: the coordination of social life* (London: Sage Publications).

Burt, R.S. (1992) *Structural Holes: the social structure of competition* (Cambridge: Harvard University Press).

Carr-Hill, R.A. (1992) 'The measurement of patient satisfaction', *Journal of Public Health Medicine*, 14, 236–49.

Dasgupta, P. (1988) 'Trust as a commodity', in D. Gambetta, *Trust: making and breaking cooperative relations* (Oxford: Blackwell).

Department of Health (1991) *Purchase of Service: practice guidance and practice material for SSDs and other agencies* (London: HMSO).

Dunn, J. (1988) 'Trust and political agency', in D. Gambetta, *Trust: making and breaking cooperative relations* (Oxford: Blackwell).

Earl, P. (1983) *The Economic Imagination: towards a behavioural analysis of choice* (New York: Sharpe).

Forder, J. (1995) 'Incentive contracts and purchaser–provider relationships in community care', paper presented to ESRC Quasi-markets conference, London, September 1995.

Gambetta, D. (1988) *Trust: making and breaking cooperative relations* (Oxford: Blackwell).

Granovetter, M. and R. Swedberg (1992) *The Sociology of Economic Life* (Oxford: Westview Press).

Hoyes, L. and R. Means (1993) 'Quasi-markets and the reform of community care', in Le Grand, J. and W. Bartlett, *Quasi-Markets and Social Policy* (London: Macmillan).

Hudson, B. (1992) 'Quasi-Markets in Health and Social Care in Britain: Can the Public Sector Respond?', *Policy and Politics*, 20(2) 131–42.

Hudson, B. (1994) *Making Sense of Markets in Health and Social Care* (Sunderland: Business Education Publishers).

Laffont, J. and Tirole, J. (1993) *A Theory of Incentives in Procurement and Regulation* (Cambridge: MIT Press).

Lapsley, I. and S. Llewellyn (1994) *Markets and Choices: contracts for care*, Paper presented to ESRC Quasi-Markets seminar, London School of Economics, 16 September 1994.

Le Grand, J. and W. Bartlett (1993) *Quasi-Markets and Social Policy* (London: Macmillan).

Luhmann, N. (1979) *Trust and Power* (Chichester: Wiley).

Lunt, N., R. Mannion, and P. Smith (1996) 'Economic discourse and the market: the case of community care', *Public Administration*, 74(3), 369–91.

Mannion, R. and P. Smith (1995) 'How providers are chosen in the mixed economy of community care', paper presented to ESRC Quasi-markets conference, Bristol, March 1995.

New, S.J. (1995) 'Supply risk and managerial accountability', paper presented to ESRC conference, *Risk in organizational settings*, London, May 1995.

Ouchi, W.G. (1979) 'A conceptual framework for the design of organizational control mechanisms', *Management Science*, 25, 833–48.

Rojek, C., G. Peacock and S. Collins (1988) *Social Work and Received Ideas* (London: Routledge).

Sako, M. (1991) 'The role of "trust" in Japanese buyer–supplier relationships', *Ricerche Economiche* 45, 449–74.

Smith, K. and K. Wright (1994) 'Principals and agents in social care: who's on the case and for whom?', *Discussion Paper 123* (York: Centre for Health Economics).

Williamson, O.E (1975) *Markets and Hierarchies* (New York: Free Press).

Wistow, G., M. Knapp, B. Hardy, J. Forder, R. Manning, and J. Kendall (1994) *Implementing Caring for People. Social Care Markets: progress and prospects* (London: Department of Health).

Index